THE WEALTH FORMULA

**BUILD WEALTH
EVEN IF YOU ARE
DOWN TO YOUR
LAST DIME**

KEN DEKKER

Printed and bound in Canada

Cover design and interior layout by www.pearcreative.ca

ISBN 978-0-9916999-0-2

DEDICATION

This book is dedicated to all the people in world that have bought into the lie that having stuff bought on credit will bring joy and fun into their lives. The shininess of our toys seems to wear out long before the payments do. We are taking our financial advice from banks whose business it is to loan out money and make large profits for share holders. Millions of dollars are spent on advertising to make us desire things and to use credit to acquire those things.

The inspiration for *The Wealth Formula* came when my father passed away at age 72. He had worked hard all his life and still had consumer debt, a large mortgage on his house and insufficient life insurance to protect those that he loved. His wife had to sell the house because she could not afford it and I bought his burial plot as he had no emergency fund. I decided right there and then that I would not leave those I love with a financial mess when I leave this world. I became passionate about understanding how to build wealth and passing that knowledge on to my children and my grandchildren. *The Wealth Formula* is especially dedicated to Candice, Sacha, Ryan, Amber, Jill and all their children who already number eight.

DISCLAIMER:

The characters in this book are fictions of my imagination and any resemblance to you or people you know is purely coincidence. The situations and life lessons are drawn from years of personal financial experience, coaching others, and reading lots of financial books and relationship books. I was once told by my business coach, Joe Stumpf, that our deepest darkest secrets about our financial and relational issues, that we believe are unique to us, are generally almost universal to the rest of the population.

The Wealth Formula is a general summary of the beliefs of the author that have helped him go from indebtedness to being a multimillionaire. This book is not to be construed as individual financial advice for you. Every person's individual situation is different and so you must seek wise legal, tax, financial, investment, insurance, and real estate advice from a professional in the industry before making major decisions. Of course eliminating consumer debt from your life is simple, may not need the service of a professional, and yet I have seen miraculous results when a debt elimination coach is utilized to help in accountability and next steps. The highest paid athletes, performers and singers usually have a couple things in common…they practice and have a great coach to encourage, correct and hold them accountable.

My prayer is that this book will be a catalyst to you to decide to make the changes that will allow you to become truly wealthy and pass that knowledge on to the next generations.

FOREWORD

With debt loads at historic highs and interest rates at extreme lows, there has never been a better time for you to understand the power of *The Wealth Formula* to change your perspective on bad debt and good debt, to change your financial world and to ultimately change your life for the better. Learn the power of compounding and leverage that can work for you or against you. The decision is yours. You can build wealth for the good money can do.

I have heard many times that money changes people. I totally disagree… money does not change people, it amplifies them. If they were stingy or greedy with a little money, they will be stingier with lots of money and if they were generous with the little they had, they will be more generous with their wealth.

Go on the journey with Sarah and David as they discover the truths about building wealth from a mysterious mentor. Use the exercises at the end of each chapter and the tools on the website to implement the strategies into your life and in a few short months you will notice a big difference in your behaviors and your life. Many have used these simple strategies to go from trying to make ends meet to being completely consumer debt free and having financial peace in a matter of a few years.

These new financial habits are simple to understand and easy to do and also easy not to do. The choice is yours. You can read this book, enjoy the story, and leave it at that, or you can do the work and change your life forever. My prayer is that after reading *The Wealth Formula* your life will never be the same. Enjoy the journey.

MEET SARAH AND DAVID

Sarah sat on David's couch with a sad look on her face, wondering what had happened to her dream of having the perfect marriage. She had expected to find peace and protection with the man she was engaged to marry; instead, she found herself sitting on a couch that he still owed money on, sullen with worry over the sea of bills spread across the coffee table. A table also not yet paid for. What were they going to do? Paying for a wedding was one thing; how could they ever dig themselves out from the weight of all this mess? Her thoughts broke as she heard her fiance arriving home from work.

"Look at what I bought today," David called from the hallway. He bounded into the a room with a huge grin on his face, a package in hand.

Wide-eyed, Sarah just stared at him in disbelief. "You don't get it!" she exploded. "We have no money to be buying anything! We are facing financial ruin…and you don't get it! What is wrong with you? What is wrong with us? Don't you love me at all?"

David's smile dropped. His eyes narrowed bitterly. "You're right," David yelled back. "I don't get it…and I don't get you! All I did was buy lunch and spend a hundred bucks on blue lights for the floor of my car. They were regularly $200, so they're a great deal. I thought you would be happy I saved a hundred bucks today, but all you do is get angry every time I spend a cent. It's like since we decided to get married, you don't want me to have any fun anymore. Sometimes I think you just don't care about me in this relationship."

Through the tears that she could no longer hold back, Sarah spluttered for words, "You are wrong; I do want you to have fun…but …" She let several bills drift from her hands to the floor.

David looked on helplessly. He gave in and put his arms around her and held her close. Words eluded her; she could only sob.

David's first marriage had fallen apart, and he was bound and determined that this marriage with Sarah was going to work. He loved Sarah more than he thought possible and couldn't imagine spending a week without her. Sarah was a soft spoken, lovely young lady. She weighed a hundred and twenty pounds soaking wet, had blonde hair, and a smile that could melt ice. It didn't take David more than one date with her to decide she was almost perfect. David, in contrast, was six feet tall, had dark skin, and a full head of thick black hair that he kept short.

David quietly said to Sarah, "I am sorry. I'm not trying to frustrate and hurt you. I just don't understand why you get so upset. It was just lunch and some lights."

Sarah's eyes were red and blurry as she tried to explain, "David, buying lunches is expensive, and I know you don't take time in the mornings to make them, so last night I packed one for you to take to work. When you buy a lunch and don't eat the one that I made, I feel like you don't appreciate what I'm trying to do."

"I do appreciate your efforts," David replied. "I'm just bad at remembering to take my lunch out of the car and put it into the truck for the day. I just get sidetracked and anxious to get started working. I don't know - maybe I can put a sticker on the car window or on my keys to remind me to put the lunch into my truck. But seriously, what is the big deal about the lights? It's only a $100. I make that in only four hours. I'll just work some overtime."

Sarah started to calm down as she explained. "I'd much rather have you with me for the four hours than have fancy blue lights in your car. I feel like I don't see you enough as it is. And it isn't four hours because that's after tax dollars. It'll actually take you about seven hours to pay for the lights."

David raised one eyebrow, confused.

"And David, it's not just today. With all the money we spend, I'm concerned that we won't have enough money for the basics, like a mortgage and food. I worry about it a lot, and seeing you just going out and spending money like that makes me panic. I had hoped when we get married we would be secure together, but it seems like we will always have bills looming over us." The pent up anxiety took its toll on Sarah, and she started crying again.

David started kissing away the tears; he finally understood. "I'm really sorry for making you feel like this. I knew you were worried about our finances, but I had no idea it was bothering you this much. From now on, I'll just ask you before spending any money."

"That's not what I mean," Sarah blurted out, "That's not even realistic. It's not that you cannot spend any money, it's that we need to set up some boundaries on what amount is okay to spend, and then seek consensus if we are going to spend more than that. Does that make sense?"

"Yeah," David agreed relieved. "Honestly, I'm really sorry. I can take the lights back tomorrow. Do you forgive me?"

"Yes I do," Sarah replied and squeezed him tightly. "I'm just so glad we got this out into the open. It feels so good to finally talk about this rather than worry on my own."

Sarah came from a caring family with little to no debt, and therefore her propensity for debt was very low. When she and David became engaged, she had only a small car loan and enough savings to pay off the five year old Nissan Altima at anytime, while still having a little money left over.

David was in a different position altogether. On the rebound, he was recently divorced. When the court proceedings came through and his ex-wife got most of their possessions, he thought, 'I'll show her.' David had a great paying job and worked lots of overtime, so getting credit was no problem. He ran out after the separation and bought a brand new Mitsubishi Lancer, rolled his old debt into the car payment that he felt he would have no problem paying, and then bought new furniture during the 'Don't Pay a Cent' Event. And of course a new big screen TV was in order. When the smooth talking salesman pointed out how low the monthly payments would be, David also purchased a surround sound system with a powered subwoofer to go with the TV for only an extra $25 a month. David started working a part time job on top of his full time job to make ends meet. Considering all the stuff he had, his friends thought he was doing great. After all, he who has the most toys wins.

Because David worked two jobs, neither one held back enough taxes off his pay cheques, and now he was behind in income tax. He also owed money to the lawyer for the work he had done on his divorce. The weight of all the debt was starting to be almost more than he could bear. It felt good to be able to forget about it and buy lunch and a few toys for his car. After all, he worked really hard and deserved it. The credit card was so high now anyways, another hundred dollars on it was not going to matter. That's what a credit card is for, right? David grew up in a family that felt debt was fine just as long as you could make the payments. The only thing was, it was getting really hard to keep up with the bills, and there always seemed to be more month than there was money. Working two jobs was helping, and yet at tax time each year, it seemed he was slipping further into debt. The tax bill was getting so large that he stopped filing tax returns so that he wouldn't owe more money. David's financial roller coaster was getting out of control.

Sarah sat on the couch in a daze. She had known David had some debt when they first started dating, but she never really realized how bad things had become until they began looking for a place to live. Currently, David was living with friends in their basement, and Sarah was still living with her parents. David assumed they would just rent somewhere cheap until they got themselves out of debt and onto their feet. Sarah hated the idea of renting because her parents were real estate investors and had taught her that when you rent, you pay off your landlord's mortgage and build wealth for him or her. She had expected that when she got married, she and her husband would buy a home and begin building equity. She wanted to pay her own family rent each month, not some landlord.

Sarah asked her parents' REALTOR ®, Yetta Dekker, to look around and see if they could find a particularly inexpensive home that needed renovations. David loved the idea because he was very handy and realized they could buy homes and flip them to help generate an income. Basically this would be like having a third job, except there wouldn't be any income tax since it would be their principal residence. Yetta worked for Keller Williams Solid Rock Realty in Ottawa, and when Sarah spoke to her about her plan, Yetta explained that they should come into the office and meet with her so that she could gain an understanding of what their goals were, explain how the real estate process would go, and explain the different levels of service that were available to them. Sarah set an appointment for the buyer planning session with Yetta for the next Saturday morning, which was the only time that she and David both had off work.

During the planning session, it became clear that the first step was for them to get in contact with a mortgage broker to see what they could qualify for in a mortgage. Yetta called one of her favorite mortgage specialists, Lynn Fraser, who also ran a financial fitness company called More than Enough, and arranged for her to speak with Sarah and David in the next hour. The couple was hoping to buy a home for approximately two hundred and fifty thousand dollars. As Lynn filled out the application for Sarah and David, she winced a little when she saw all the debt. A credit check confirmed the worst - David's credit score was very poor and he had a lot of debt which caused him to not qualify for a mortgage at all. While Sarah made a small income, her credit score was great because she only had a car loan and she made her payments on time every month. Lynn explained to David how the back taxes, late payments and the bills he had co-signed for his ex-wife were hurting his credit score. "On top of all this," Lynn noted grimly as she swiveled in her chair, "the 'Don't Pay a Cent' credit is also harming your credit score."

"But it's not due yet!" David exclaimed.

Lynn explained that the credit at the furniture store was under a year old, so that affected the score, and then the credit limit was set at $1400. He had spent all of that, plus there was a $99 administration fee, which meant that he had a $1499 balance on a $1400 credit limit. "Anytime you are near or over your limit," she said, "you lose more points on your score." The late payments on his minimum payments on the credit cards were also dropping his score, even though they were only a few days or weeks late on average.

Seeing David's downcast expression, Lynn tried to encourage him. "Don't worry, David. All is not lost. By taking certain actions over the next few years, you'll be able to pay down your debts and improve your score." She laid out a plan for him to do just that and then explained that at this time, they had one of three options. First, they could wait until their finances and credit score improved; second, they could see if they could get someone to co-sign the mortgage; or third, they could buy a house at a value of $125,000 or lower. As that is what Sarah qualified for by herself.

David and Sarah really did not want to rent and they knew that they would never find a home for under $125,000, so they decided to ask Sarah's parents to co-sign for the mortgage. Sarah's parents loved her dearly as their only child, but their views on debt just didn't allow them to be comfortable with this idea. They also felt Sarah and David weren't ready for the responsibility of taking on a mortgage of that size when their finances just weren't under control. Sarah was disappointed; however, she understood her parents' wisdom and didn't push the subject.

A few weeks later Yetta called Sarah and David and explained that an old home located in the country had come on the market at a very low price. The house needed just about everything updated: new electrical, a proper bathroom, insulation, windows, a septic system, drywall, flooring; the list went on and on. Since the home was a much more affordable $50,000, they decided to go look at it with Sarah's parents to see if it was something they could fix up. However, after seeing how bad a shape it was in, David felt it might just be too much work for him to tackle alone and the cash needed to do the upgrades would be almost impossible to come up with. Sarah's father Michael offered to help him and suggested that they go ahead with an offer conditional on inspection by a professional. Yetta mentioned that a purchase plus improvement mortgage may also be available that would give them a final mortgage based on the renovated value so they had to finance the renovations until they were complete and then the remainder of the mortgage would be advanced. After the inspection confirmed the amount of work to do, and also confirmed that the foundation and structure were sound, they decided to go ahead and buy the house. After a quick closing, they began the work immediately as their wedding was now only eight months away.

Their new house had white vinyl siding on about sixty percent of the outside and and a huge summer kitchen, garage, and workshop area that were just ship lap wood, with the paint peeling off. Many of the windows were broken; the roof leaked and sagged under the weight of a hundred years. The floors were extremely sloped, and the stair case had a significant lean to it so one had to hold onto the low railing to go up or down. The smell of years of mould and mildew hovered over the old carpets along with the smell of urine from the mice that had overtaken

the rooms. The smell was almost too much to handle, and yet this was
Sarah's and David's new home.

<u>Friday</u>

I feel so insecure about my financial safety. The fear of not having a place to live and this load of debt has given me a heaviness I have never felt before. I am already facing so many challenges with planning the wedding, and just getting used to the idea of being married, that the debt stress is putting me over the top. It is nerve wracking to think that I can't trust David in this aspect of our lives.

A few weeks ago I had a meltdown, and it was awful and embarrassing, but I think I had a breakthrough with David. I think he finally got a glimpse of how I am feeling, and how the bills aren't something we can just shrug off or leave stacked in a corner. I think this message really hit home too when we talked to our mortgage broker, Lynn. It became so clear how our debt is limiting our future.

I think David sees all this now and believe he truly wants to change our money situation. Not sure he has

the skills to do it. We have made a
good start though, with buying this
crazy ramshackle old house. It is
going to need some serious TLC -
we have to use a ladder to climb up
into the second floor and I can't go
into some of the bedrooms yet until
the carpet is ripped out because it
stinks so much like pee. Thankfully,
David is great with a hammer and
tools...as long as he gets his morning
coffee first :)

I pray someone comes into our lives
to help. I know David is a proud man
and wants to support us. It would
be great to go to Mom and Dad with
our money problems and just borrow
or do whatever they advise, and
yet David needs to feel I trust and
respect him. He will need to decide
who and when he is ready to ask for
help.

MY DECISIONS AND ACTION ITEMS

What is keeping me awake at night?

Who do I look up to as a mentor?

Who do I know that is an expert, or knows someone that is, in the areas of:

Investing:

Debt elimination:

Insurance:

Tax:

Real Estate:

Estate Planning:

Law:

Relationships:

THE NOT-SO-PERFECT BUY

Work on the new house began slowly. For starters, the house was a sixty minute drive from Ottawa, limiting work to days off, which were few and far between for David as he worked two jobs to help make ends meet. As he and Sarah began ripping out the carpet and removing ninety plus years of accumulated wall paper, it became apparent that a very big job lay ahead of them. Since it was already November, the first and most pressing need was to insulate the outside walls as they had nothing in them except three layers of wood. The next challenge was to rewire the electrical as the house had knob and tube wiring, which prevented the home from being permanently insured until it was completely removed. Soon David discovered that all the interior walls were constructed of a single layer of tongue and grove planks which were toe nailed into the floor and ceiling, meaning there were no cavities to pull electrical wires through. The solution was to tear out every interior wall. David decided he was okay with this since he wanted to change the floor plan and had to install a bathroom anyways. After a day of Saws All and black coffee, David stepped back and surveyed his work. Now that he had cleared all the interior walls, it was time to put new windows and doors in the outside walls. Mercifully, the heating bills began going down once the exterior was all fixed up.

One day while working on the house, Sarah and David decided to take a break and go exploring in the loft over the summer kitchen, garage, and workshop. They had so far ignored this huge area of the house because they were focused on the main floors. As David made his way up the steep staircase, wiping spider webs out of his face and hair as he went, Sarah followed closely behind. "Yick," grimaced Sarah. "No one's been up here in a long time!"

David was surprised at how easily the trap door opened. After they climbed up, he examined the door and discovered a unique weight and pulley system attached to a rafter. Someone had installed it so that it opened easily and stayed open at a very wide angle. A previous owner had spent some time putting that mechanism together.

"David! It's huge up here," exclaimed Sarah.

Pulled from his daydream, David surveyed the room and was taken aback by the size and height of the loft. He had no idea from looking at it from the outside that it would be this large. David stepped onto the floor wondering if the old structure and boards could hold his two hundred pound frame. As he gingerly walked along, Sarah at just over a hundred pounds ran all over the loft marveling with excited oohs and ahhhs. The floor bounced up and down as she delightedly ran from treasure to treasure. The house was sold as an estate sale and apparently had come with a number of tools and items that were left in the workshop garage area.

The first thing Sarah found were some glass balls with pointy ends, almost like oversized Christmas balls. A pinky semi-clear liquid floated in them. "Hey, David? What are these?" she called out. Examining them further, she noticed that the metal wall bracket to hold these decorative balls had a label that read: Throw at the Base of Fire. "Oh neat!" Sarah murmured "Hey David? I think I found some kind of old fashioned fire extinguishers."

David, however, caught up in his own excitement barely heard. "Look what I found!" he bellowed.

Sarah made her way over to where David stood admiring two overgrown lanterns. Like the ones you take camping, except these were thirty six inches tall. The pair was covered in dust, looking like they had been there for forty years. Next to them were ten foot boxes covered in bird droppings and more dust. Peeling back the lids, David found that they contained enough siding to finally finish the back area of the house. "This is wonderful!" exclaimed Sarah with a delighted laugh. "Who knew all this was up here all this time?"

As they went over to a raised section over the summer kitchen, they found an assortment of vintage metal Tonka trucks. Sarah surveyed the length of the attic. "Wow," she mused, "it's big enough up here to build an indoor basketball gym." She smiled wryly, "This'll be great for when we have our three boys your mother is convinced we'll have!"

David grinned and said, "Let's worry about making the house livable first."

As they rummaged through more boxes and various odd pieces of junk left from years gone by, David moved a large sheet of wood and was surprised to find behind it, leaning against a wall, a bicycle built for two. There was something different about this old bicycle. It was bright red and had virtually no dust on it compared to everything else they had found. David was mesmerized. "Sarah, mind giving me a hand to get this bike down the stairs, please?"

He went down the steep stairs first as Sarah slowly passed down the bicycle. Once outside in better light, they marveled at the condition of the old bike. There was not even a scratch in the paint or a speck of rust on the chrome handlebars and rims. Sarah ran to get some cleaning cloths anyway and David headed to the workshop looking for a tire pump and an oil can.

"This bike is beautiful," marveled Sarah out loud as she rubbed minor traces of dust off the handlebars. "I wonder who it used to belong to?"

"Maybe to the couple who lived here before us," suggested David as he put down the oil can and spun one of the wheels.

"Could be," Sarah replied undeterred. "But why would they leave it here? Why not sell it or give it to their kids? It looks like something from an old black and white movie. I have a feeling it's really old."

Satisfied with their work, the couple stepped back and stared at the bike. David flicked the rag over his shoulder. "It really does look brand new, doesn't it?" he asked.

Sarah nodded her head.

They put the bike away in the garage and went in to continue their work constructing new interior walls and leveling the floors. At the end of the day they kissed each other goodbye, drove back to their respective homes, and fell into bed utterly exhausted. Both dreamt about stepping out of their completed house on a warm summer day and laughing confidently as they took the bike out for a ride.

Sarah and David were so excited that the wedding was approaching quickly. They were determined to remain pure until their wedding night. Fortunately between working so much, living in different towns and all the work on the house there was little time left over for alone time. It was actually amazing how much time Michael had spent with David on the house and for that matter how many church families and friends would stop by for a day or afternoon to help in any way they could. The house renovations slowed considerably and would have to wait as a lot of time was now being taken up preparing for the big day; finalizing the guest list, dress fittings, tux fittings, writing their vows, scouring garage sales looking for decorations for the hall, going over changes to the menu, and having their final pre-marital counseling meetings with their pastor.

The months had flown by, and now weeks became days, and days became hours, until the minutes and seconds finally came, and then each second seemed to drag on for an eternity as David waited at the front of the church and Sarah felt faint standing at the back with the music about to begin and her to take that long walk down the isle with her dad. When the first chords of the song filled the sanctuary, she walked forward clutching her father, thinking her legs had gone to rubber and that she couldn't walk on her own. David looked up eagerly as his bride made her entrance. His chin dropped down in awe as he caught the first glimpse of her. A tear ran down his face as suddenly he realized that everything in his life up until that point ceased to matter and this was the dawn of a new beginning and a new life for him and Sarah.

The night screamed by with speeches, camera flashes, and hugs from all their guests. Then suddenly the weeks of stress were all over, and David and Sarah were in the car waving goodbye to friends and family. It was time for David to take his new wife for a week to relax and to enjoy one another's company. Because they were so in debt and had no money the usual sand and sun destination for honeymooners would have to wait and they decided to spend a few days at Niagara Falls, and then the rest of the week on a lake where friends had loaned them their cottage for five days.

It was a clear morning. The air was breezy, and few people were out on the lake. As they lay languidly on their towels, the couple could hear disgruntled seagulls fighting over floating sandwich remains from another cottager.

"What are you thinking about?" Sarah asked David.

David lazily opened one eye, his hand on his forehead to block out the sun. "Nothing." He nestled deeper into the sand.

"What?" Sarah flipped onto her belly and pushed up her sunglasses. "Okay, what are you thinking about right....now?"

"Nothing."

Sarah lay back down unconvinced. "And...now?"

"Nothing."

"What?" Sarah exclaimed, sitting back up. "How can you be thinking about nothing? You have to be thinking *something*."

"It's easy. I sit here enjoying the peace and quiet, the hot sun, and I go into a stress-free place where I think about nothing."

"Wow," said Sarah mystified, "Seriously? I'd love to join you there; I'm always thinking about something."

David laughed and said, "You can't join me because then it would no longer be nothing." Sarah made a mock pout and flopped back down with a smile on her face.

Picking up on the clue, David asked, "What are you thinking about?"

Sarah snuggled in close and put her head on his shoulder. She drummed her fingers absentmindedly on his chest and murmured, "I can't get that red bike out of my mind."

"Really?" said David raising his head with surprise. "You too? I've been thinking about it this week. We never went for that ride we said we were going to take."

"Yeah," Sarah continued. "It's been months, and the weather has warmed up. We've just been so caught up with the wedding. It was fun, wasn't it? The wedding. But, I have to say, I am so glad it's over and that we're finally married."

David hugged her tighter. "Yeah. Once we get back, we get to officially move in to our home, and married life really begins."

"Hurrah!" chirped Sarah happily.

"The day we get back to the house, I'd really like to go for a ride on that bike with you," David said.

"Deal!" Sarah said. She sat up and shook the sand from her hair. Noticing his eyes on her, Sarah smiled coyly. "David?" she asked innocently, "What are you thinking *now*?"

David pushed her over into the sand.

After their week of honeymooning, they drove to their new matrimonial home. And what a treat that was: no flooring in yet, no plumbing or running water, and one extension cord for power from the electrical panel outlet. David laid out the queen size blow up mattress in the dining room area, as this was the one area he had managed to clear construction dirt, dust, and materials from. He hung up some old sheets over the two doorways to try to keep the dust from blowing into the room and hung one over the window.

"I guess this is home for now," he said self consciously.

Sarah made the best of it. "It's like being at the turn of the century," she insisted. "We're pioneers. I can get water from next door, and..." She looked around. "Well, I guess we'll have to use the corner store's bathroom, or just use a bucket for now."

David hung his shoulders hopelessly until Sarah punched him good naturedly on the shoulder. "It could be worse, chum! At least we have each other."

He snapped out of his mood and grinned at Sarah, "What a trooper you are. I am sorry it's taken so long to get the house ready. Now that we live here, I'll have time in the evenings to work, and I'll get a bathroom and our bedroom done first."

"It's okay," said Sarah. "As long as we have each other I can put up with a lot. Let's get some sleep so that tomorrow we can go for that bike ride." She bounced up and down amusedly. "You know this blow up mattress is not half bad. It's all the fun of camping without the annoyance of mosquitoes and having to set up a tent!"

"Let's hope this house won't leak when it rains," groaned David.

The next morning Sarah awoke before David. She was so excited about being in their new house and going for a ride on the bicycle that she could barely sleep. Sarah got up and made some coffee and toast for David. This was an unanticipated challenge as she only had one plug, so coffee came first then the toast after.

After their simple breakfast, Sarah said, "Let's go!"

"Where?" asked David sleepily. The coffee hadn't yet kicked in.

Sarah smiled, "For a bike ride silly. Remember?"

"Oh yeah," said David with a big grin. Last night he had dreamt about the bike again and so was surprised he had forgotten.

David got up from the makeshift table, two low benches with a sheet of plywood on top. He went outside, rolled the bike out of the garage, and straddled the front seat while a shorter Sarah tried desperately to get on without tipping over. After a few feeble attempts and one close call, they were both on and starting down the road.

When David tried to turn on a right hand corner, Sarah felt like they were going to tip so she leaned to the left. The bike started to shake a little as David leaned harder to this right and turned the steering wheel further to the right. Sarah then leaned even further to the left. David realized that he was not going to make the corner and a truck was coming towards them in the left lane. He pushed on the brakes, the bike promptly tipped, and both he and Sarah toppled hard onto the ground. David quickly helped Sarah up and brushed off the little stones stuck to her skin. Little drops of blood started to appear once the stones were removed.

"I think that's enough for one day. Let's walk home and get you cleaned up." David suggested.

Sarah rubbed her rump and winced. "Good idea."

David picked up the bike and to his amazement saw there was not a scratch on the bike. "Huh, how about that?" he wondered as he walked it and Sarah home. As they reviewed their seemingly failed attempt, they discovered that they had fallen down because they were not working together. "I guess that is pretty important when riding a tandem, eh?" asked Sarah.

"Well," said David, "We both thought we were helping; just, we weren't communicating enough, that's all."

David put the bike away in the garage and went in to clean and bandage his and Sarah's scrapes.

It was now back to work and back to usual as David went to work each day delivering grocery products as a truck driver and Sarah worked in food services at a hospital. Each night they tackled an hour or two of construction, threw some food together, and fell into bed exhausted.

One Thursday night David came home all excited. He pushed open the front door to find an equally distracted Sarah. She twirled happily in the dining room. "How do you like them?" she asked.

"Like what?" David asked.

"My new shoes, silly." Sarah mussed.

David looked down and replied, "New shoes? Oh they're nice. Uh…" he took off his jacket and continued cautiously. "How much were they?"

"That's the best part!" Sarah excitedly replied, "I got them at half price for twelve dollars."

"Wow! That *is* a great price!" David replied enthusiastically.

Sarah looked a little sheepish as she completed the truth. "Well actually, I did have to pay $50 for the first pair."

"What?" exclaimed David indignantly.

Sarah explained, "They had a buy one, get the second at half price sale. Don't they look great?"

"Yes, but that's not the point," David retorted.

"Oh, yes it is," said Sarah defensively.

David sat down on the air mattress and sighed. "I guess that's okay." His face lit up as he remembered and he jumped back up, grabbed a slice of bread, and stuffed it into his mouth. "I can't argue about a great deal," he muffled walking around the room. "Especially since I found such a good one on a snowmobile for next year. It's last year's model and with two hundred dollars down, there are no payments until next summer. Then it's just $299 a month."

Sarah piped up nervously, "My dad always said, 'Don't buy toys with credit…Pay cash.'"

David snapped. He whipped around to face her. "I'll never have the cash if you keep buying shoes!"

Furious, Sarah snapped back, "What do you mean? I paid with cash from *my* pay cheque."

"Then fine," David said determinedly. "I'll put $300 a month from my pay check in a separate account so I can buy the sled when I have enough money saved up."

"You don't love me!" Sarah wailed.

David threw his hands up dramatically in the air. "No way. You're not using that one on me again! I love you plenty. I just want to have some fun and go sledding with my buddies. They all bought sleds on credit."

"Well we're not them!" cried Sarah. "We have so much debt from your past, and we need to get on the same page."

Deflated, David sat back down. "You're right," David replied. He put his head down and sighed.

Relieved he was listening, Sarah calmed down somewhat and quietly said, "I'll return the shoes tomorrow."

David also calmed down and said, "No, that's okay. We just need to be on the same page. It's like riding the bike. If we don't work together on our money and finances, we'll crash and get hurt."

Sarah sat down next to him on the bed and put her head on his shoulder. "I know I am usually the one who is tight with the money, but I find this hard too. I'm not used to having so little. I used to pay my bills and necessities and spend money on things I wanted with the cash I had left over. Now we have to pay all these bills and interest, so there is not enough left to buy the odd thing. It's hard to accept."

"I know," said David quietly as he wrapped one arm around her. "It'll be tight for a while, but we can dig out. I know we can. It's just going to be hard until then."

He rubbed his neck with his free hand and looked out the window. "We still have a few hours of daylight left. Do you want to try out the bike again?"

"I guess so," said Sarah hesitantly as she gingerly ran her fingers over the scabs on her knees from the last attempt. She wasn't exactly in the mood to go, but a glance at her husband's face told her he could use some fun.

It was a beautiful evening. The air was warm with a slight breeze to keep the mosquitoes away. They got on the bike, and this time Sarah promised to lean with David and David promised to go easy on the corners. Off they went, and it felt like they had ridden a bike together all their lives. Faster and faster they flew as the two peddled together, becoming sensitive to the other's movements. The wind blew in their hair, and the tall oaks lining the roadway protected their eyes from the brightly setting sun. They waved to new neighbours working in flowerbeds and teenagers shooting hoops in their driveways. Every now and then, they passed a family of bike riders or mothers anxiously chasing after children on tricycles. There was little traffic at this time of evening. Exhilarated by the swift speed they had discovered, David and Sarah felt they could bike forever. David commented over his shoulder, "It is so easy to peddle when both of us are working together, isn't it?"

Sarah heartily agreed.

After about an hour, they stopped to take a break. David looked at the sunset and said, "We'd better think about heading back as it will be getting dark in about an hour and a half."

"You're right," replied Sarah. "And what a perfect evening it was."

Just as they were about to turn around, David pointed. "There's a car just ahead pulled over, and it looks like the driver may need some help."

As they closed in on the vehicle, David could not figure out what kind of car it was. He was a car enthusiast and thought he could recognize most cars from a distance, but not this one. It was a gleaming graphite gray, and sleek. A two seat convertible. David admired the lines and thought to himself that it must be a European roadster. As the couple neared the car, it became apparent that it had a flat tire. A man standing beside the car, hands on his hips, was giving it a little bit of a frustrated look. David greeted the man and asked if he could use some help.

"I sure could," said the man good naturedly. "I have never changed a flat tire before and I probably am not dressed for it."

David looked a little closer and saw the man was meticulously dressed from head to toe. His hair was brown, perfectly styled and cut with a fashionable waviness. He had on a perfectly pressed shirt and a patterned tie that picked up the lilac coloured pinstripe in his navy suit. His black leather shoes and belt matched perfectly, and there was not even a scuff on the shoes. His fingers were clean and his nails manicured. It was obvious that he was no blue collar worker.

"My name is Zane," said the man as David introduced himself and Sarah.

"You're not from around here?" asked David.

Zane replied, "No, I'm from Ottawa and was trying to take a scenic drive when I got a flat tire in one of those giant potholes. I must not have been paying enough attention to the road as I was listening to a great book while enjoying the evening's coolness with the top down."

David looked a little puzzled. "A great book?" he asked.

Zane replied, "Yes, I was listening to *Today Matters* by John Maxwell, and I was working at memorizing the twelve items to attend to each day."

David breathed out in surprise and dragged his foot in the gravel. "Sounds boring to me," he said hesitantly. "If I was in a fantastic car like this, I'd be ripping down the road with rock music blaring."

Zane piped up, "Oh, sometimes I do, but most of the time I prefer to listen to books as I drive. It serves a dual purpose," he explained. "I call it my university on wheels. I've listened to twenty four books since I bought this car two years ago. It is part of my growth plan. I figure if I listen to and or read one self help book a month, I will become a much better person over time, and most of the time I have to drive somewhere anyways, so why waste the time?"

Sarah interrupted the two, "What is a growth plan?"

"Oh", said Zane, "a growth plan is like a calendar of planned events and daily or weekly events that I schedule in that will help me grow as a person, become more valuable as an employee or a better business person and ultimately make more money in less time is my goal. Most people put into their schedules things like; doctor's appointments, holidays, special events, hobbies and the like and yet very few schedule in special trainings they want to go to in the year, the number of books and type of books they will listen to or read, mentors they want to find, and courses they want to take to improve themselves. As a matter of fact most people never pick up another book after their formal education except for a novel or magazine."

David took advantage of the pause. "Speaking about your car, what kind of car is it? I've never seen a car with this much leather, especially with the black and red pine striping. The Trident symbol on the front is very cool as well," he couldn't help adding.

"Oh!" said Zane. "It's a Maserati. It's made in Italy and I just love the lines and feel of it. It also has a Ferrari engine that produces 390 horse power. I have changed the exhaust and added a performance chip so it now probably produces over 400 horse power."

David's eyes widened as he asked, "Does it have a super charger?"

"No David," he replied smiling, "This is a naturally aspired V8."

David wondered whether there would be room for a turbo under the hood because he could only imagine how much power this Maserati Spider could produce with a turbo kit. Zane must have read his thoughts as he said, "It is a bit hard to not use too much power and get speeding tickets as it is. I would hate to see how much trouble I could get into if it was super charged."

David nodded as he remembered the last few tickets that had caused his insurance to sky rocket the last time he renewed. He had promised Sarah to follow the speed limit as they couldn't afford another ticket. "Well, let's get your tire changed," David said as he rolled up his sleeves and knelt on the ground.

Sarah leaned on the bike's handlebars and smiled at Zane. David had gone straight to work; Zane had only to stand back and watch. As he worked at jacking up the car, David bashfully asked, "What would the payments be on a car like this?" At the moment his car payment was $600 per month and he figured this car must come in at about $1800 per month.

Zane smiled a little and replied, "I don't believe in payments on anything except houses and investments. I bought this car with cash. It was eight years old when I bought it, and it had only 12,000 miles or about 20,000 kilometers. The car cost less than a third of the price of what it cost new. I buy all my cars used and let someone else take the depreciation. On this car someone else lost about $10,000 a year in value, plus they probably financed it because they thought it was normal to always have a car payment. If you add interest on top of that, this car probably cost the first owner about $14,000 a year without any gas, insurance, or maintenance costs. I paid $38,000 for it and will keep it at least another ten years."

"I see," said David a little surprisedly as he started to lower the car. This was not the answer he had been expecting. He'd never considered this method of buying cars before. "I'll just put your tire in the trunk and you are set to go."

"Wow, thanks a lot," said Zane. "How can I repay you guys for helping me out? I may have been out here for a long time if you hadn't stopped to help."

"It was nothing," David replied."Just help someone else in return sometime."

"Done," said Zane with a big smile on his face.

David and Sarah watched in awe as the little sports car flew off and became a dot on the horizon in just a few seconds. Sarah shoved David lightheartedly in the shoulder and wryly remarked, "You can pick your tongue up off the ground now."

David looked worried. "Was it that obvious that I was shocked at how nice a car that was, and that he doesn't believe in payments on anything except a house and investments?"

"Umm...Yes." Sarah laughed sarcastically, as memories of what her parents had taught her came rushing back. "We better get going as it is now already dusk." She got back on the bike and steadied it with her feet on the ground, waiting for David to join her. Instead, she felt herself being lifted up and deposited on the ground beside the bike. "What?" she asked confusedly. "David!"

David had jumped on the bike and was awkwardly trying to speed back down the road without her. Except, the lack of weight on the back end caused it to bob dangerously, making it appear as though it was going to flip. Laughing, Sarah chased after the bike, her threats becoming increasingly creative. "If you don't come back here now, I'll put salt on your toast tomorrow morning!..Or, toothpaste..in your socks!" David just hooted in reply, until the bike hit a rock and he toppled into the bushes. "Wyyaaa!" he shouted in surprise as he flew through the air. Sarah laughed so hard she thought she was going to be sick.

That night, with Sarah's arms tangled around him, David lay awake for a long while. He had a hard time going to sleep as he was so annoyed with himself for all the consumer debt he had collected in such a few short years. This new little financial truth he had learned today made his former mistakes seem that more foolish. As he drifted off to sleep he thought of the four long years before he would have his two year old car paid off, and he sighed as he recalled all the interest he would be paying in the meantime.

<u>Thursday</u>

I cannot believe how quickly time has gone by. Our wedding was incredible. I can't believe how smoothly everything went and how much fun the actual day was. Much more fun than the planning! It was tough working with the budget my parents gave me. But then, even if it had been twice or three times as much, I still would have found it difficult picking out the dress, food, location, flowers, deciding how many people to invite, etc. As much as I loved being the bride and feeling special, I am so glad that is all over. It was so nice to get away on the honeymoon and relax! And what a blessing to be loaned a cottage for five days as we really didn't have the money for an elaborate honeymoon. That dream will have to wait until a later anniversary, I think.

David and I have spent a lot of time working on the house lately. Sometimes it seems like that's all we do - work at work and then work on the house. Doing it together

makes it special, though. Plus,
we've been taking a lot of bike rides
during our breaks. It seems working
together in life and on the bike sure
makes things easier. I think even
more than twice as fast and easy.

Met Zane today. He is this neat
businessman who drives a really
cool car. Forget what kind it was. I
could never admit that to David. You
should have seen my husband's drool
dripping on the ground as he changed
the flat tire. Wish we could see
Zane again. David seemed to get it that
borrowing money is for homes and
business investments only. He really
was shocked that a sharp guy like
Zane only buys used cars with cash.
It is so amazing seeing David getting
these little realizations. Maybe there
is hope after all that we can turn
things around!

MY DECISIONS AND ACTION ITEMS

What audio book do I have that I can listen to in the car? Can I borrow one from a friend or library?

Are there books on a growth plan and when can I schedule time to build my growth plan?

What debts do I regret or new cars do I regret having purchased in the past?

What am I sick and tired of being sick and tired about?

What decisions or action items am I going to do and by when?

A NEW GPS...FIRST GEAR

The next morning it was like David was a new man. He woke up early, made a mental list of all the things he planned to do that day, pulled on some pants, and followed the smell of coffee into the kitchen. He sat at the breakfast table with Sarah and announced, "I am sick and tired of all this debt; we need a plan to dig ourselves out of this mess. I'm just not sure how to go about it."

Sarah agreed. "I'm so glad you've come to that decision." She set the pot on the table. "I've been worrying and not sleeping at night because I'm so anxious about all of the bills. I keep dreaming these awful nightmares where we lose the house and don't have enough money to feed ourselves. Sometimes we have to move in with Mom and Dad. Other times we're hiding in this old garbage can in an alleyway." She laughed nervously, "And then we have to keep dodging the police because they are all hunting us down to pay off our loan from the 'Don't Pay a Cent' Event." She wrapped her hands around her mug and shivered. "It's a terrible feeling."

David half smiled but felt badly. "Oh Sarah, I wish you wouldn't worry so much. You know I'm a hard worker, and I'll support you for as long as I live," he responded with as much confidence as he could muster.

"Yeah, I know, but I want to see you once in a while as well," sighed Sarah.

A week or so went by, and things were pretty much status quo. Sarah was home early and starting dinner when the phone rang with dreadful news.

"Sarah, I've been in an accident," said David.

Sarah's heart lunged up into her throat. "Are you okay?" she gasped.

"Yeah, I'm fine, but work has fired me. They said my driving record made me too much of a risk." The line grew quiet. "I'll be home soon."

Choked with anger, embarrassment, and fear, Sarah searched for the only positive thing she could think to say. "I love you David," she mumbled, more to herself than to her husband.

When David arrived home an hour and a half later, Sarah was a mess. She had all their bills out on the kitchen table and tears were streaming down her face. David came in silently, his head down as he pulled up a chair. Sarah knew he felt he failed as a man. She knew he needed reassurance that she still believed in him, but right then she was just not willing to give it. She enjoyed withholding it, if she was honest. He was just lucky she resisted the urge to unleash all her anger and frustration on him. It took all her might not to rant furiously at him. How it was his fault they were so in debt to begin with, and how he should have been more careful at work because now his accident had made things just that much worse. David sought her eye, but Sarah stubbornly focused on the bills. She had not signed up for this. She deserved better, and she knew it. They had only been married for a month and a half, and already Sarah was starting to feel trapped.

Finally David stopped waiting for a response. Perhaps he knew a positive one was not coming, and he pulled her into a hug, more for his own reassurance than hers. Sarah wanted to push him away but felt too tired to fight. Instead, she hung her arms limply around his shoulders. "How are we going to pay all of these bills on my small salary David?" She tried unsuccessfully to keep the edge out of her voice.

David held her tight and said, "Don't worry Sarah. I'll figure something out, and I'll work more hours at my other job until then."

Sarah got up and went to lie down on their bed. David stared out the window wondering what exactly had happened to them.

As the weeks went by David spent every evening trying to find another job and worked as much as he could for his part time employer. It wasn't enough. The bills kept piling up, and he and Sarah were fighting more and more. He felt like an absolute failure and resented her silences almost as much as her accusations.

One night David ran out of the house as there was nothing to eat in the refrigerator. He didn't have the nerve to ask Sarah what was for dinner and so jogged across the yard in the rain to the corner store to pick up a six pack of beer, a pizza, and a movie.

He was in the checkout line when he saw Zane coming into the store. Just like last time, he had on an immaculate suit and his hair was perfect. "Hi Zane," greeted David.

"Oh hello, David! Fancy meeting you here," replied Zane.

David smiled, "I live just next door."

"Oh do you? Well how about that! And how are things going, David?" Zane inquired.

David explained their recent circumstances.

"That's hard," Zane agreed. "Are you open for some input?"

"Sure!"

"Great! Well, then put down the beer and movie and let's go have some pizza with Sarah. My treat."

"That sounds great," David responded.

As they walked outside, David looked around. "Where's your car?" he asked.

Zane pointed to a black car, "I brought the Infiniti today."

David paused mid step and questioned, "Really? You have more than one car?"

Zane smiled and explained, "Of course David. I can't drive the Maserati in all weather conditions so I have this Infiniti M35X for the winter. It has all wheel drive for those snowy days."

"It's really a nice car!" exclaimed David.

"Yes it is," said Zane, "and fully paid for as well. Cars just seem to drive better when you don't have any payments on them."

"I wish I didn't have any payments right now," said David.

Zane nodded knowingly, "I understand. Let's go see Sarah and chat about things."

Sarah was delighted to see Zane coming into the house with David. Zane smiled at Sarah and said, "I understand you are in a bit of trouble since we last met."

"That's an understatement," agreed Sarah wryly. She gave David a guarded look.

Zane continued, "David said it would be okay to chat about financial matters. Are you up for that as well?"

Although a little embarrassed to be discussing their financial situation with an acquaintance they barely knew, Sarah was also relieved, "Oh boy, am I ever!"

Zane pulled a chair up to the makeshift table and looked over at David who was pulling plates out of a crate. "The first fact about your problem is we need to FACE the issue."

Sarah cut in, "What do you mean FACE?"

Zane continued, "Well, FACE is an acronym for Financial Awareness Creates Empowerment. First, you need to track where your money goes and then create a budget which will allow you to spend everything on paper before the month actually begins. That way you know where every penny is going"

Sarah jumped in again, "I hate budgeting. It's so depressing. I'd just rather not spend anything."

David could no longer remain quiet, "I know. That's why there's no food in the refrigerator."

Seeing the scathing look Sarah shot David, Zane spoke up. "Now guys remember, you are on the same team. You need to work together. It is just like riding that fancy bike built for two."

"You're right," David said. "Sorry, Sarah."

Sarah gave a slight nod in David's direction and motioned for Zane to continue.

Zane continued, "First, David, you need to get another job even if you don't like it. It's easier to get a better job when you have one to start with. Second, stop buying anything that is not an essential need. Right now that is food, gas, and the bare maintenance items for safety reasons. Cut the beer and the movies, you can live without those for the time being. Third, pay the minimum on all your bills and don't go behind on the house or utilities. You need to keep Sarah feeling secure."

Sarah snorted.

Zane ignored her comment and continued. "Fourth, sell things you do not need anymore for as much as you can get. Fifth, track every dime you spend so that you can see where your money is going. This tracking is where the FACE comes in." He looked over at Sarah. "Even if David had not lost his job, this tracking is vital so that a proper budget can be made and spending habits adjusted. Without a proper budget, it is easy for anyone to end up in this situation."

Sarah busily wrote notes as the others polished off the rest of the pizza.

"Incredible," Zane mumbled, "that was the best pizza I've ever eaten." He wiped his hands on his napkin and stood up. "Well, I should be heading off now. I have to be up at five thirty."

"Really?" asked David. "Why do you have to be up that early? You said your work doesn't start until nine."

Zane smiled. He seemed to always smile when there was a lesson about to be taught. "Yes that's right, my employment starts at nine am and there is much to do before work."

"Like what?" questioned David. He just couldn't understand the way Zane thought. "I seem to only have time to work, work around the house, and watch T.V."

Zane smiled again, "You're like a lot of people, David. The rituals we have become habits. Most think of a habit as bad, and yet if you have good habits we call them 'disciplines'. Both are habits. We are very habitual people. Most go to church each week and sit in the same chair, or at dinner we like to sit in our spot. My habits are just like rituals. I get up at 5:30am, so I can get most of my habits done before work. I listen to an educational program while working out for half an hour, then I pray and read my Bible, then shower and get dressed. I have a fruit smoothie with protein while I plan out my day. I spend fifteen minutes reviewing my finances and then I take time to reflect for thirty minutes."

"What do you think about?" Sarah blurted out.

"All kinds of things," Zane answered, "like ideas or vision for my life, friendships I need to work on, and acts of kindness I can do."

David sighed, "Wow, I'm tired just thinking about it all."

Zane continued, "Then I leave the house at 8:15 so I'll be twenty minutes early for work if traffic goes well, and on time if I run into a snag."

Sarah shook her head, "Yes, but with all your rituals surely you must not have freedom to do what you want to spontaneously."

Zane's voice became soft, "Oh Sarah, that's where you are wrong. Disciplines, or good habits, are like a good budget. When you are disciplined you are actually freed up to do what you want, when you want, with the rest of your time, or in the case of the budget, your money." He looked at his iPhone. "I really have to run now as it is getting late."

Sarah hugged Zane impetuously and asked, "Can we meet again?"

Zane smiled, "Yes, I am positive our paths will cross again."

"When?" David quizzed.

"Not sure." Zane responded. "Have you heard the saying when the student is ready the teacher will appear?"

David nodded.

"I believe the teacher is always there, and the student only sees the teacher when the student is ready. Well, I'm off. Have a good night, you two."

"Good night!" Sarah and David called out simultaneously. They glanced at each other cautiously and watched the LED taillights of the Infiniti fade out of sight.

Things have gone from bad to worse.
David lost his job a few weeks ago.
I've been feeling completely lost in
this sea of debt, and I've really been
resenting David for getting us into
this situation. Zane was a surprise
visitor today at the perfect time.
David and I are really struggling.

His Advice:
- FACE: Financial Awareness
  Creates Empowerment
  - Track every nickel we spend
    for a month
  - David get a second job even
    if it's not a good one
  - Sell everything we don't
    need
  - Pay minimum on all bills
  - Keep food, house, and
    utilities a priority
  - Don't buy anything unless
    absolutely necessary or
    safety issue
- ***Habits can be good or
  bad. Our habits make us who
  we are and we can change our
  habits

I am starting to learn that less is more. I actually get more quality time with David now that the cable TV and cell phones plans are gone. We are reading, playing cards, and praying together a lot more. I am also beginning to feel more loved by David. I am going to have to forgive him soon, so that I can move on and stop lording his mistakes over him. He doesn't deserve the way I've been treating him. Just not sure how to go about it...

Am I willing to FACE my spending habits?   Am I willing I track every dime I spend for one month??

Do I work within a zero balance budget?

Am I willing to go to www.wealth-formula.com to download or print the budget form?

FIRST GEAR... WHEN THE GOING GETS TOUGH, THE TOUGH GET GOING.

The following weeks continued to be difficult. David took a job driving and loading a garbage truck. He was dirty and exhausted every day when he came home from work, and yet still managed to do his part time job. Picking up garbage was grueling work; however, even though it was hard, he felt productive and was therefore happy. Sarah started selling almost everything that wasn't tied down. She polished the two lanterns and fire extinguishers she and David found in the attic. She learned about Ebay and sold lots of tools and antiques they had found in and around the house. The lanterns went for $500 each and the fire extinguishers sold at $50 a piece. The Tonka toys were actually in great shape and sold from $50 to $100 each. Sarah sold everything they didn't absolutely need, the couches and coffee tables in storage...even the TV and stereo went. When David weakly protested, Sarah snapped that it was better to eat than watch TV. Cable services and cell phones were the first to go. It was hard to believe that these seemed like necessities and yet were not. The two items alone reduced their monthly bills by $160.

Sarah was delighted; there was food in the house, which was a good thing as David was eating like a horse after loading garbage all day. As she began to relax, so did David, and they stopped bickering. Sarah was reminded of how considerate David was even when he was tired, and she appreciated the sacrifices he had made so uncomplainingly. David on his part felt he was no longer measured by his shortcomings; he began looking forward to coming home from work again.

Sarah continued to sell off things they could live without, but for some reason could not bring herself to sell the bicycle built for two. David seemed to agree. Every weekend he and Sarah would go for a long ride. It was a great way to relax: they got exercise, and it gave them an opportunity to talk about how things were going. One special Saturday, Sarah packed a picnic lunch and a blanket as a treat. It had been several weeks since they started tracking their spending and changing their habits.

When David got up Saturday morning, he hugged Sarah and said, "Let's go for a bike ride."

"Already planned," said Sarah.

The two had breakfast and David packed the lunch into the basket on the front of the bike. They rode for what seemed hours and probably was when they came to a park on the St. Lawrence River. The embankment had a rocky three foot drop to the water below with large shady oak trees lining the river. The couple found a perfect spot and spread out the blanket. David stretched out contentedly as a team of ducks quacked happily in the water below.

As Sarah began arranging lunch, David heard a familiar sound. "Shhhh! Wait a sec.," he motioned to Sarah as she clanked the tupperware.

Sarah looked puzzled. "What?" she asked.

"Listen!" he said, his grin growing wide.

"What?!" she asked.

"Can't you hear that exhaust note?"

"No," Sarah laughed.

David explained, "It's a Maserati!" as he jumped up to go look in the parking lot. Sarah grinned and shook her head in disbelief as she watched David run over the hill to the parking lot. She snuck a strawberry. Then she fed a few sandwich crumbs to the ducks. Minutes later David returned with Zane. "See," he said, "I knew I knew that exhaust note!"

"You're unbelievable!" exclaimed Sarah laughing. "Hi, Zane!" She invited him to join them for lunch.

Zane jumped at the invitation, "Don't mind if I do. I was out for a drive and stopped at this park looking for somewhere to buy lunch."

"What a coincidence," said Sarah, "We have plenty for all three of us."

Over their sandwiches, the couple caught up with Zane on how well they had done over the three weeks since they had last been together. David and Sarah had stopped eating out; they now prepared lunch and coffee thermoses in the morning as they were getting up an hour earlier to make breakfast and plan their day.

"It's actually really peaceful and nice," Sarah finished off.

"Yeah," added David. "When I start my morning early like that, I don't feel stressed rushing to work, and my day just seems to go better. I don't get annoyed at every red light anymore and I don't feel the need to speed. It's like I'm able to take on the challenges of the day with more awareness or something."

Sarah nodded in agreement. "And it's nice to start my day spending time with David and planning out our goals together. I have more of an idea about what we both want for our lives. It's helped me to get to know him more, actually."

"That's fabulous!" Zane cheered with a jubilee like only he could muster for someone else's success.

As they packed up, Zane said, "It sounds like you are ready for the next step."

"Just a minute," said Sarah as she rummaged through her picnic basket and pulled out a journal and a pen. "Since we first met, I have been writing out our thoughts and ideas and have been tracking our spending in this journal."

Zane smiled as he said, "That's great Sarah. The next step is a small one, although a very important one."

"What is it?" asked David curiously.

Zane continued without skipping a beat as he had gotten quite used to the interruptions of his enthusiastic students. "Well, it's small and yet may be both the easiest and hardest step to do because it goes against what most people do and think is wise."

"What is it, what is it?" Sarah pressed like a little school girl with her pen poised to write it down.

Zane smiled, "Save two thousand dollars as an emergency cushion."

"That's it?!" exclaimed Sarah.

"Yeah, that's it," Zane replied. "All the rest of the steps depend on this first one."

"You've got to be kidding!" exclaimed David. "The first secret to being wealthy is save two thousand dollars?"

"Yes that's it," said Zane smiling amusedly at their confusion. "You see most people have good intentions, and they try to pay off more than the minimum on their debt. Then, an emergency happens, and then the credit card comes out for 'just this one emergency,' and the habit of using credit is perpetuated. You need an emergency fund so that you can break the habit of using credit."

David couldn't understand Zane's logic. "It doesn't make sense to have money sitting in the bank when we have debt at 18% and 26% interest, does it?"

Zane replied, "Well at first glance no, and yet to break your habit, yes it does. It's important to be aware that an emergency is not Christmas sneaking up on you, or a two for one sale, or we-ran- out-of-food-because-we-did-not-budget-properly. Speaking of budgeting, I know it is a dirty word in most people's vocabulary." He settled back on the blanket and threw a stray crumb to the ducks.

"Budgeting is simply telling your money where to go." Zane borrowed Sarah's journal and sketched out a rough series of numbers. "Here's a sample of a simple budget. You'll notice that there is a zero at the bottom. What that means is that every dollar we plan to make in the month we plan to spend in the month. Right now all your money will be used for debt servicing, living expenses and savings towards your cushion. Please note that giving and saving are at the top of the budget form. They are not at the bottom as an afterthought if there is any money left over."

MONTHLY BUDGET

Income		Expense		Goal
David	5000	Givings	100	10%
Sarah	2000	Wealth Building	0	10%
		Savings	500	5%
		Car		
		Mortgage		
		Food		
		Electricity		
		Oil		
		Clothing		
		Personal Care		
		Entertainment		
TOTAL	+7000		- 7000	
			0	

Sarah studied the budget and said to Zane, "I can see why we have savings in our budget, but why is there a giving line when we are so tight right now?"

Zane smiled again as he flipped through their notebook. "You think you are so tight right now," he said kindly, "and yet there are still many places that you are spending discretionary money. I can see on your tracking. David, you are buying soda a few times a day, and Sarah I see Starbucks and Tim Horton's on your list a couple of times a week."

Sarah spoke up defensively, "Yes, surely we deserve a break every once in a while?" She glanced at David. He shrugged his shoulders in confusion and nodded his head.

"I agree," Zane nodded, "So do your budget, and if there is money left at the bottom for meals and entertainment, then go ahead and spend those dollars on coffee and drinks."

David had to interrupt. Usually Zane's advice was encouraging and made so much sense. This, on the other hand seemed so blatantly foolish, he was catching himself irritated with his teacher. "But Zane, how can we be giving money away when we have debt at 28%? That just seems crazy! We work hard for our money. I work two jobs for crying out loud. I don't feel I need to give any of that money away!"

Sarah nodded in agreement.

Zane smiled again. "David, can I be frank with you?" he asked patiently.

David nodded his head.

"Back when I was in your situation, my finances were so bad, I was borrowing on my Visa to pay the minimum payment on my MasterCard. I had consolidated my debt four times, and each time my habits didn't change, so I just kept spending and got further in debt and racked up the credit cards. What I found was that when I gave away 10% of my income, I became the master of my money and money no longer mastered me. I gave a 10% tithe to the church I started attending and my life changed. The car did not break as often, I got a raise at work and then a promotion. It just seemed life got easier. Now I am not saying you need to give to a church. If you attend one, I would say that is where you should give, and if not you can give it to any of the other great causes like YouFeedThem.com, Big Brothers or Sisters, cancer research, the Heart and Stroke Foundation, hospital building campaigns, AIDS research, etc. By the way, you don't give to get, yet that is exactly what happens. It's a universal principle like gravity, it exists and affects me whether I believe it exists or not. Love is another one. If you want more love, give more love away; it does not diminish. When you give love away, it increases. Try giving money away and see what happens. Test me on this!"

Zane glanced at his iPhone. "David and Sarah, I should be going. I have an important date tonight. Before I go, Sarah, please write in your journal this website address   www.wealth-formula.com. I have some tools on there that you can download. The first one to download is the budget form. You can download it as a PDF, which is a simple, free way to print it, or you can download it as an Excel spreadsheet if you have Microsoft Excel on your computer."

"Oh, that's helpful," Sarah said excitedly. "I have Excel on my work computer."

As Zane got up from the blanket, he picked up the garbage bag and said, "Enjoy the rest of your day, guys, and enjoy your ride home. It's great to see you out on your bike."

He slam dunked the garbage into the public garbage can and was heading back to his car, when David called out, "Will we see you again?"

"That's up to you, David and Sarah," Zane hollered back, tossing them an encouraging smile over his shoulder. And with that, he disappeared over the hill into the parking lot, and then they heard that wonderful sound as Zane quickly accelerated the Maserati out onto Highway Number Two.

As the sound quickly faded into the distance, David turned to Sarah and said, "That guy is really different, but I like him. I don't totally understand his advice, and it doesn't always make sense, but I'm learning so much. When do you think we will see him again?"

"I don't know, I don't know," replied Sarah with a puzzled look on her face. "He said it was up to us and yet he has never given us any contact information."

They spent the remainder of their wonderful afternoon on the blanket watching the ships go by. It was hours before they jumped on the bike and headed home. As they were lying in bed that night Sarah said, "You know, David, that was one of the best dates we have been on in a long long time."

"Yes it was," David agreed. "And to think it didn't cost us any more money than we would have spent anyway to eat at home." He kissed the top of her head, "Night, Princess."

"Night, David," Sarah mumbled sleepily.

Monday morning came quickly and yet Sarah had a new bounce in her step. She enjoyed working with spreadsheets and looked forward to starting in on their budget. At lunch Sarah easily downloaded the form and began filling out the columns. It was difficult to pin down specific amounts, but then she remembered she had been recording that tracking list for the last couple of weeks in her journal. It was then a simple task to transfer their spending into the budget. She finished the spreadsheet up on her last break for the day and printed a copy to show David that evening. Sarah always got home first and made dinner for her and David. That night she planned to make his favourite meal; she suspected talking about finances would make him feel a little stressed and she wanted to help him feel comfortable.

David came through the door grumbling irritably, "I need a shower!" before heading upstairs without even a kiss or a hug. Sarah suspected it was a bad day at work. He came down fifteen minutes later with a fresh smell and a fresh attitude.

Sarah smiled at him holding up a plate of steak. "I made your favourite!" She had turned off the lights and lit a few tea lights.

David plopped into his chair and rubbed his hands in anticipation, very hungry after a long, active day.

As she passed him the caesar salad, Sarah asked David about his day. She always enjoyed getting updates on what went well, things about his job that he enjoyed, and his hilarious retellings of funny events. She found it gave her a lot of insight into how he viewed life and helped her feel close and intimate with him.

David started to grimace. "I guess it isn't so bad really," he said, "but I was ticked when it happened. It was before lunch break, and I was loading garbage into my truck in Greely. The hopper was full, so I turned on the hydraulics to press the garbage into the truck. As I was watching the garbage compact, I heard a pop sound like a plastic bag or balloon popping. I wasn't quick enough to move away as a bag of sour milk exploded all over me. I got drenched in sour milk from head to toe."

Sarah tried to keep a straight expression and failed miserably as she burst out laughing. David's face dropped and turned cold. Sarah had a habit of laughing when shocked, which meant often at the wrong time, especially if someone hurt themselves. David's earlier irritation revived, and he waited impatiently to calm down. Sarah by this point couldn't stop laughing as the picture of how shocked he must have been was too vivid in her mind. Sarah's chuckle turned into one of those belly laughs that hurt, and now David couldn't help laughing at Sarah laughing, and the two laughed until they were gasping for breath. David wiped the tears out of his eyes, explaining how he had to go back to the depot and rinse his hair and change uniforms since he couldn't stand the smell of himself. When David said this, Sarah gave up. She ran for the bathroom as she was laughing so hard the tears threatened to run down her thighs.

They finished their meal on a great note. David turned on the coffee machine and loaded the plates into the dishwasher. Sarah called him back to the table. "I have a surprise for you," she chirped.

David rubbed his hands together in anticipation again. He loved surprises, especially gifts.

Eager to make the procedure as painless as possible, Sarah quickly pulled out the budget and began to explain it to David. David's eyes instantly glazed over. He didn't exactly enjoy staring at numbers on paper and had been expecting something a little nicer than a budget.

As Sarah went on, David got quieter and quieter and then suddenly exploded, "I hate this! You are taking control of my life! There's nothing in the budget for me."

Sarah couldn't believe it. She had gone through all this trouble to put the budget together and had taken so much care to be sure she cushioned the way she approached him with it so that he wouldn't get upset. She didn't know what else she could possibly do to make this man happy. And anyways, she couldn't help judging, it was his fault they were in so much debt to begin with. Unable to take it any more, Sarah growled back. "That's not true. Your car payment, lawyer payment, furniture bill, stereo bill, *and* visa bill are *all* in the budget."

David glared back at her in disbelief. He didn't understand why she was jumping all over him. He knew that it was his debt that had them in this mess, but that didn't mean he could never spend another cent on himself. She was the one who arranged the budget. He would have given her more spending money if he had calculated it himself. Why couldn't she be more reasonable?

David's silence left Sarah shaking with anger. "I don't like this any more than you do, David, but we have to make changes. We are going to drown in this if we don't." She realized the intensity of her voice and took a deep breath to calm herself down. "Besides," she said after a few moments, "I don't understand why you are so upset. I thought you wanted me to make a budget. Why are you mad at me so suddenly?"

Realizing her confusion, David tried to explain, "That's not what I mean. I feel so restrained. There is nothing for upgrading my car, nothing for my new sled, nothing to blow just going out with the guys!"

"Blowing money? What about me? I need a haircut for Pete's sake! I've been cutting my hair at home for the last month. Every day I look in the mirror and see a frizzy wreck looking back at me. Do you see me complaining?" She knew she was pushing him too far, but she couldn't resist throwing in one last jab. "You're so selfish! It's all about you and your toys!"

David hunched angrily in silence as what Sarah had said began to sink in. He hated to admit it, but she was probably right. Okay, she wasn't probably right, she was right. He had complained more about their financial stress than she had, while she was the one working so hard to get them out of it.

He sighed and pulled her chair over to his. "You're right, princess," he said, his hand rubbing the back of her neck. "I am being selfish. This budgeting is hard, and I know you must have put a lot of thought into it. I have worked really hard at staying positive; sometimes this just feels too overwhelming."

A little light came back into Sarah's face. "I'll tell you what," she said. "How about you add or change as much as you want? The only stipulation is that the budget is a zero balance budget; so, that means if you add something, we have to change some other numbers so that the column still balances out to zero."

"Okay," said David a little revived. "That sounds fair. All I really need is twenty dollars a week to spend on what I want, so that if I want a coffee or to go to the movies I can do it. Otherwise, this budget will feel like a jail sentence. Once the $20 is gone, I won't spend any more unless it's in the budget."

"I can understand that," agreed Sarah.

"Well," declared David as he examined the spreadsheet, "we don't have a lot of playing room, do we?"

Sarah nodded knowingly.

He began to see why she was so upset; she probably felt as discouraged as he did. "Well…okay, how about we take $10 a week from meals and entertainment, $5 a week from food, and $5 a week from clothes?" asked David.

Sarah replied, "But then we will only have $20 a month for clothes."

"I know," said David, "and right now we have so many clothes, the only thing we really need are boots for the winter."

Sarah started to protest and then bit her tongue. He was right; she didn't really need anything right now. Or for the next year if she was really honest. She thought of all the clothes in her closet and realized if she gave away half of them, she would still probably have enough. It is fun to shop and buy new shirts, but it is more for entertainment than anything. She could learn to find ways to do that for free. In truth, it would probably be liberating to learn to resist her shopping impulses. This might be really good for her.

"Okay. We can do that," conceded Sarah. "Thing is, I think I should also get the same amount to spend on what I want too. Otherwise, I can see myself getting resentful."

David grimaced as he looked at the numbers and agreed. "It's only fair," he said. "Okay, what if we take $15 a week from meals and entertainment, $10 a week from food, and $5 a week from clothes? That way we each get $15 a week, and we can use some of that money for our entertainment and food. We'll just have to get creative. Maybe we can eat at your parents more often," David laughed.

Sarah, beginning to enjoy the interaction, answered, "You're right, David. I think I can live with this budget…Do you?"

"It'll take a bit to get used to, but I think we can do it," he answered. David leaned back in his chair and a slight frown crossed his features.

"What is it?" Sarah asked.

David leaned forward and put his elbows on the table. He slowly took a sip of coffee and placed the mug gently back on the table. "You have been really amazing about our financial situation, Sarah. I know that it's been really hard on you. And you've been really great about making adjustments and still keeping it cheerful. I know too that sometimes you resent me for the money we owe. I know that I brought a lot of debt into this marriage, and I feel really bad about it; I just am wondering how long you are going to hold it against me. You don't say anything about it very often, but I suspect that deep down you are still angry with me."

Sarah slumped forward on the table too and played with her mug. "You're right," she admitted and sighed. "Usually I tell myself it doesn't matter, that we all make mistakes, and I can just shrug it off. After all, I know how hard this has been on you too, and you've been so amazing by working so hard and in making all these changes. Sometimes, though, when I'm frustrated about our money, I can't help feeling resentful."

"What can I do?" David asked. "I keep asking myself what more I can do, and I can never come up with anything. I know I messed up before, but am I failing you now? Today? Is there something you want me to do about it that I haven't done?"

Sarah shrugged helplessly. "I don't know what you can do. I don't usually feel this way," she said in her defense. "Just sometimes."

"The thing is, Sarah, when you say things like you did earlier, about *my* bills, I feel like less of a man. I feel like you don't respect me, like you think I am always going to make a mess of things. It is hard to get motivated to make changes when my wife is just waiting for me to make another mistake."

"Oh, David, I'm sorry," moaned Sarah leaning into her elbows and putting her arms over her head. "I am sorry for making you feel that way. Do you forgive me?"

"Yes, I do, honey," replied David, rubbing her back. "But now, do you forgive me for the debt I brought into this relationship?"

Sarah paused for a moment, toying with her mug. She knew what she should say, and she also knew if she said it right now, she wouldn't keep the promise. She just didn't know how to forgive him. Right now she *felt* like she forgave him, but she knew that next time he seemed selfish, she would resent him again.

Then Sarah remembered what she heard one Sunday at church. The pastor told the congregation that forgiveness never comes naturally, that it is always a choice. Sometimes a daily choice. Sometimes a choice to be made minute by minute. She wouldn't always feel like forgiving him; she would have to keep making the choice to forgive if they were ever going to move on.

"Yes, David," Sarah said. "I do forgive you. I want to release us both from the past."

David hugged her as he suspected she had just gone through a battle of her own. "Thanks, honey. I am going to make you proud with this budget. Thanks a lot for putting it together. It's terrific, and I think it'll really help us meet our goals."

Sarah beamed with the recognition. Already she felt so much lighter. She slapped his knee affectionately, "You're welcome, David."

"Oh, and Sarah, I'm sorry too for losing my cool over the budget. I'm in unfamiliar territory," David apologized. "I'll try not to do that again."

"I forgive you for that too." Sarah squeezed his knee and stood up. "Now," she said triumphantly, "let's paint the second coat on the bathroom and then go to bed."

"Sounds good to me princess," yawned David as he headed up the stairs with a full belly and a head full of figures.

Weeks went by and everything seemed fine until it was time to make the mortgage payment. Sarah did a double take as she noticed there was not enough money in the account. "How can this be?" she asked David. "I've been spending within the budget. Have you?"

"Yes," responded David with an indignant look on his face. "It sounds like you are accusing me of spending money that I shouldn't have."

Sarah tried to calm David down, "No, I'm not blaming you. I just can't figure this out."

David's eyes widened, "I've heard your dad say many times that businesses and people most often have enough money, they just struggle with cash flow. I don't know what he means, but do you think this is a cash flow problem?"

Sarah lowered the statement and tucked it in the filing system they kept near the phone. She replied, "Could be, I guess. Let's give him a call; he always loves to help."

Sarah picked up the phone and explained their new budget system and the problem. Sarah's dad was delighted with what David and Sarah were up to and suggested that they get together for lunch after church the next afternoon. He could explain what to do as they did have a cash flow problem. Sarah hung up the phone. "David, you're right. It is a cash flow problem, whatever that means."

"Is this an emergency?" asked David.

Sarah wrinkled her nose, "It sure seems like it to me."

Now David started to smile as he loved to be the guy with the solutions to their problems. He leaned comfortably against the counter and crossed his arms. "Well why don't we take some money out of the emergency savings account to cover the short fall, and then when you get paid, we'll put it back plus what is in the budget for this month."

"You know, that's a great a idea," mused Sarah. She shook her head and smiled broadly. "What would we have done if Zane had not explained about the emergency fund? I guess we would have been late on the mortgage or asked the bank for a higher credit limit on our Visa, although the last time we asked and our Visa was at the limit, they said no." She grinned. "It's great not having that kind of stress on our shoulders anymore!"

That Sunday afternoon, after a lunch of grilled cheese sandwiches and tomato soup, Sarah's dad Michael sat down with the couple while Sarah's mom Ruth cleaned the dishes. Michael explained that although they were going to get enough money in the month to cover expenses, it might not always come in when the bills are due. In other words, the flow of cash did not meet the needs of the bills and thus created a cash flow problem.

Sarah and David listened intently while Sarah wrote notes in her journal. Michael marveled at the change in the couple. He had offered them learning opportunities many times before, and David and Sarah seemed bound and determined to learn the hard way.

Michael explained that most people solve poor cash flow planning by using credit or overdraft protection on their chequing account. The problem with overdraft is that hundreds of dollars each month can go to fees and interest. Most banks charge a fee for every cheque that takes the balance below zero, and when one gets paid his or her paycheque, the balance goes positive for a short time. That is, until the next cheque takes it below zero again for another fee and more interest. When businesses do this because they don't have enough cash reserves, they can miss payroll, the first sign of a problem and the spiraling down of the business over time. Most businesses fail because they are under capitalized with enough cash to make it through cash flow crunches.

"I am so proud of you for budgeting and saving a cushion," Michael exclaimed.

Sarah and David relayed how they had found the bicycle built for two and how they had met Zane while out for a ride. Ruth nodded her head, clearly impressed by the benefits of his influence. "Sounds like a very wise man," she acknowledged.

"We think he is, and we hope to keep meeting with him," said Sarah.

"In the meantime," said Michael as he pulled out a blank piece of paper, "let me show you a simple cash flow sheet I designed for us a long time ago. I'll use the numbers in your budget and bank statement to make it easier to understand."

Pay Cheques		Bills Due		Balance in Chequing
				+500
Sarah	1000	Mortgage	2000	-500
		Electricity	100	-600
David	2000			1400
		Visa	300	1100
		Groceries	200	900
		MasterCard	200	700
		Oil Bill	200	500
		Groceries	200	300

Sarah	1000	Saving	500	800
		David Car Payment	600	200
		Sarah Car Payment	271	-71
David	2000			1929
		Groceries	200	1729
		ESSO	500	1229
		Cash (Meals & Entertainment)	100	1129
		Groceries	200	929
		Insurance	300	629
		Bank Charges	60	569
Sarah	1000			1569

Michael pointed out, "David and Sarah, notice how when I draw this out on a timeline sheet, there are two times during the month that your account will be negative, as well as at the end of the month?"

The couple nodded.

"It looks pretty good to have $1569 left, and yet on the first of the next month you have a mortgage payment and an electricity bill that will make you go negative again. Also note that this month was a three pay period for Sarah, so you are starting with a little more next month compared last month. Something that you could do to help would be to ask the bank to change your mortgage payment to every two weeks and for the payment day to be the day after David's pay. This will even out cash flow somewhat and result in you paying your mortgage off sooner because you are making two extra payments a year compared to the one monthly."

Sarah looked confused. "That doesn't make sense, Dad."

Michael continued, "Sure it does Sarah. Look, if you pay monthly, you make 12 payments. If we multiply that by 2 we would have 24 payments. Correct?"

"Uh...right?" questioned Sarah, still not understanding.

Michael was undaunted, "Okay, now how many weeks in a year?"

"Fifty two."

Michael was loving this. "Right. Now, divide that by two week intervals and you get 26 payments. You see 26 payments compared to 24 payments, and you won't even notice it because it falls on David's pay weeks."

"I'll go to the bank tomorrow!" David announced. "This is fantastic. It is the kind of thing we'd never think about on our own." He leaned in closer at the table. "You mentioned there are other things we can do?"

"Oh yes," said Michael with a glint in his eyes. "Keep your cushion in your chequing account right now. As long as you are only spending money in your budget, the emergency fund will start covering any cash flow issues as it builds up. As long as you don't need to use it, you will always have a cushion in your chequing account and should never have to pay overdraft again. You may also be able to put the car payments onto a bi-weekly payment that lines up with Sarah's pay week. This should iron out some of the speed bumps that cause you to go behind each month.

Once these changes are made, you may also want to adjust your discretionary spending based on projected cash flow requirements. This means one week you may need to spend less on groceries or entertainment, and the next week you may be able to make it up. The whole point is that knowing and putting on paper what you are going to spend each month is the heart of a budget. Knowing when during the month you are going to get money and when you are going to spend money puts you in total control."

Sarah hugged her father, "This is awesome Dad. I now have a peace about our finances that I've never had before. I always lived in fear of spending money. Thanks a lot!"

David chimed in, "Yes, thank you! This now makes total sense."

Michael enjoyed seeing the light come on. "You're welcome. It was my pleasure. Say hi to your friend Zane when you see him again."

On the way home David was quiet so Sarah asked, "What are you thinking about?"

"It's weird," David said slowly. "For the first time in my life, I'm not worried about my credit and am totally motivated to pay it off. You know, I was talking to John at work, telling him how I'm not happy about our loans. He said, 'You're not living life to the fullest if you aren't maxed out on your ability to borrow.' I said, 'You've got to meet my friend Zane.' Then I realized we have no way of reaching Zane to find out what the next step is."

Sarah nodded her head, "I know, and I was thinking the same thing. We usually see him when we go for a long bike ride. Let's plan a long trip for next week."

David agreed, "Sounds good to me princess."

The week flew by as David and Sarah continued to work on their house after work each night. On Saturday morning they packed a lunch and off they went for a three hour bike ride. Unfortunately, they didn't see Zane.

Another week went by, and still no Zane. Weeks passed.

David and Sarah had gotten more comfortable with their budget by this point and the savings for their cushion was up to $1500. Sarah came home with a new dress one day and hid it in the closet hoping David would not notice it when she wore it for the first time. David had started eating lunch out again as it was just easier. Each week they would go for a ride on the bike and each week there was no sign of Zane. At the end of the month Sarah was checking the bank statement when she noticed that the cushion was not as big as the previous month. It had slipped to $1,100 and they had not had an emergency. That night she cornered David

"Have you been spending money not in the budget?"

"Why do you ask?" questioned David. "Have you?"

"I asked you first," Sarah snapped.

David knowing he was caught admitted, "I may have bought some lunches on my debit card that I forgot to track."

"What?" Sarah asked sharply.

"Yeah I did it. I thought we were doing so well that it wouldn't matter."

Now it was Sarah's turn to confess. She sighed. "I know what you mean. I bought a dress a couple weeks ago and hid it in the closet."

"Really?" gasped David, looking like a cat that just swallowed a canary.

A long pause ensued as David and Sarah stared at each other with their heads slightly turned down and a discouraged look on their faces. Sarah broke the silence, "David we need to be accountable to each other. We were doing so well."

It was David's turn, "I know we were Sarah. Let's go for a ride and see if we can find Zane."

After another three hour bike tour and no sight of the Maserati, David and Sarah returned home discouraged at not finding their friend. They quietly got ready for bed and slipped under the covers.

"Hey Sarah."

"Yes David?"

"Do you really watch every dime we spend?"

"I sure do," piped up Sarah, "I really want to hit the $2000 mark for our emergency fund."

"Okay!" David said with new resolve, "I'll take any overtime I can get, and until we reach that goal, I won't take out any spending money."

"Me too!" said Sarah, "We can do this thing." She kissed David passionately and then rolled over to go to sleep.

Four short weeks later, Sarah ran out to meet David as he arrived home from a Friday overnight shift at his extra job.

"Sarah why are you so excited?" asked David.

"We did it David! We did it."

David was confused. "Did what?" he replied, thinking they had won the lottery. Then he realized how much had changed. They didn't play the lotteries anymore, not since Michael taught them that the odds of winning are so low it is really just a voluntary tax. One that only the middle class and poor seem eager to pay. He couldn't help smiling when he realized how much he'd learned over the past few months.

Sarah was now jumping up and down. "We reached the two thousand dollar mark in our emergency fund!"

"That's great!" David explained. He caught Sarah as she leapt into his arms and wrapped her legs around his torso.

Sarah kissed him hard on the lips and asked, "Do you feel like going for a bike ride?"

David yawned and replied, "Let me have a nap and then I'll be up for it. You know I just finished a double shift."

"I know," said Sarah, "I just got really excited. We'll go in a few hours."

Time ticked by very slowly as David slept and Sarah tried to stay quiet and keep busy around the house. The hours passed by until David meandered sleepily down the stairs and asked, "Anyone up for a bike ride?"

"You bet!" Sarah yelled from the living room. "I already made us a snack and filled our water bottles."

She entered the room and hugged him from behind as he helped himself to a glass of water. "Hey, you know David, you are looking much slimmer since you cut out the soft drinks and fast food."

"Thanks for noticing," David beamed as he puffed out his chest and sucked in his stomach. You know, he thought to himself, picking up garbage sure is a tough job but my fitness level sure has improved.

Saturday

We went for a wonderful picnic at the St. Lawrence River. We were surprised by Zane, and he shared lunch and ideas with us. He seems to show up just when we need him.

His advice:
- Save $2,000 emergency cushion
- Do up a budget on www.wealth-formula.com
  - Put giving and saving at the top, then bills and necessities
  - If money is left over, the last category to get money is eating out and entertainment

Monday

Ack. Introducing the budget to David did not go over as smoothly as planned. Poor boy thought he was getting a present! We had a big fight, and both of us felt attacked. David calmed down once we decided he could manipulate the columns to something he was more comfortable with. Realized I am really resentful of him for all this debt, and it is

eating me up. I chose to forgive him
and am releasing us both from the
past. I don't exactly know how to
forgive, but I think it means I have
to keep deciding to forgive him over
and over until I feel it.

Sunday

Our account went negative again,
and Dad explained that a zero budget
could still have cash flow problems.
Changing our payment schedule for
the mortgage and car payments has
solved the problem. We are paying
them off quicker with the extra two
payments that bi-weekly payments
bring.
We go biking many times and still have
not seen Zane.

Friday

Putting our emergency fund into
our chequing account may have
been a mistake as we have both
been spending a little extra money
and our emergency fund has slipped
from $1,500 to $1,100. We were
doing so well, I guess we just got
complacent with our money. David
agreed to work extra and we both

agreed to not spend any discretionary money until we hit the $2,000.

<u>Saturday</u>

Today, after only four weeks of concerted effort we finally made our $2,000 emergency fund after a few setbacks and some new resolve. Mom always said a setback can be a setup for a comeback if we are determined.

Do I have a cash flow problem?

What payments can I change to line up with pay periods?

How much money have I spent in overdraft, bank charges and interest over the last 12 months?

Do I have an emergency fund and how much is it?

SHIFTING INTO SECOND GEAR

Sarah and David jumped on the bike and headed out. Over the past few months they had become really proficient at riding as a team. They decided to head towards the St. Lawrence River again, and as they rounded the corner of their house, David exploded with excitement as he saw that beautiful Maserati parked out front of the corner store.

David almost jumped off the bike before he had brought it to a stop and let Sarah off the back. They parked it against the side of the store and ran in to see if Zane was in there. Sure enough, they found him paying for an extra large meat lovers' pizza. He smiled at the couple and said, "I've just not been able to get this fabulous pizza out of my mind for the last couple of months, so I had to come and get some. Would you like to share with me?"

"Would we?" exclaimed David, "It's been over a month since we've had pizza."

Sarah laughed and shook her head. "Men," she said. "Hey, why don't we go back to our house to eat it? I have a two litre bottle of coke in the back of the fridge that I've been saving for a special time like this."

"Sounds good to me," Zane replied as he paid for the pizza and the three walked back to the house.

After dinner, the three sat down in the living room on fold up lawn chairs to discuss how things were going.

Sarah was the first to blurt out, "We have accomplished the $2000 dollar emergency fund!"

"And it wasn't easy," David added.

Zane nodded that knowing nod, "I knew it wasn't going to be. Yet, you wouldn't be ready for the next step if you hadn't been able to do this first step."

"We did have some struggles," Sarah admitted, slapping her hand for emphasis on David's knee. He smiled sideways and trapped it in place. She grinned and continued. "The first thing I don't understand is why you have percentages beside the top three categories in the online budget form that I downloaded from your website."

"Good for you for noticing." Zane applauded her. "As you complete the next steps, the goal is to increase these top three to a minimum of 10%, 10% and 5% until all your debt is paid off. This way as your income increases, these items will increase as well."

David jumped in. "What's the difference between wealth building and savings? Aren't they the same thing?"

Zane smiled, "Your savings account is for saving up for large purchases, while the wealth building account is an account that you will never withdraw money from."

"What?" asked David startled. "It might as well be another giving category if we can't spend it."

Zane continued, "You're sort of right, David, this is wealth you're going to leave behind for your children and your children's children, or for charity as a legacy fund."

"Wait, I don't understand," David interrupted again.

He looked so confused, Sarah and Zane couldn't help but smile. Clearly, this concept was an entirely new one. Sarah got up to put on the coffee maker.

Zane smiled, "You will when we talk about wealth building and retirement in the future."

Sarah pulled three cups from the cupboard and filled one with cold water for Zane. "Speaking of the future," she said, placing it down on the table in front of him, "we had no way to reach you."

Zane looked at Sarah with that big smile again, "You're right; I really am hard to reach. Remember I said that students would find the teacher when they were ready?"

"Yes?"

"Well," he leaned back in his chair, "you'll find me when you are ready for each step."

"I'm not going to pretend to understand," said Sarah laughing, heading over to the sugar bowl. "But, we'll take all your advice while we can! The second thing we had trouble with was we only spent money within the budget but still ran out of money. My dad called it a cash flow problem."

"Your dad is wise," Zane mused.

"We figured it out with his help."

Zane smiled. "I knew you would. On the wealth formula website, you'll find a cash flow tool."

David took his coffee gratefully from Sarah and added three heaping tablespoons of sugar. "Pass the milk, babe?" he asked. He pushed the last of the pizza in his guest's direction. "Zane, I hope the next step is to build wealth like you have. I want to find out how to get the best return on any investment we are able to make in the next few years. Right now, I'd have no idea what to do with any extra money. All I can think of is just leaving it in the bank where it is safe." He smiled regretfully at Sarah, "And we both know I'd think of a few things I'd like to get for us, so it wouldn't stay there for long!"

Zane smiled, "Funny you should ask that David. Today's step is all about how to glean the best return you can make."

David put down the milk. "I'm all ears."

Zane paused and stared at him curiously. "That's funny you don't look like you're all ears!"

Zane chuckled good-naturedly while the other two groaned and shook their heads.

"Okay, okay, terrible Dad jokes aside," said Sarah, "I have my pen and journal ready. Give me a couple of pages worth, Zane!"

Zane spoke slowly and purposefully. "Pay off all your consumer debt."

There was a long pause.

"That's it?" David and Sarah questioned in unison.

Zane loved this part. "Yep, that's it! Let me explain. Do you understand the difference between before and after tax dollars?"

"Not fully," David admitted.

Zane continued, "The $20 per hour you make is before tax; after tax, that is about $14 per hour. When you make money on investments, the same principle applies. You have to pay tax on the money you make." He went to the sink to fill his glass with more water. "The interest you are paying on your debt ranges from 7% on Sarah's car loan to 28% on your department store card. What would you say if I said I have an investment that pays 28% and it is tax free?"

Sarah almost feel off her seat, "I'd say tell me what it is!" she exclaimed.

Zane loved her enthusiasm. "It's called paying off your department store card." He took a long drink of water and thumped his glass on the counter for emphasis. "And the best part is the 28% is tax free because it's savings and not income."

"Okay, I am starting to get it," David nodded.

"Let me give you an example to drive this point home." Zane sat back down and leaned in towards David at the table. "Could you get me some paper and a pen so I can write it out?"

Sarah responded, "Sure but why not use my journal? That way I can keep your example and we won't lose the piece of paper."

"Good call," David said.

Zane started talking faster in his excitement. "First of all, you need to know the rule of 72. The rule of 72 states that when you divide 72 by your compound rate of return or interest on an investment, the answer will be approximately the number of years for the investment to double."

He paused to glance at his friends' blank stares and continued, "You both look puzzled, let me explain. If you are getting 6% rate of return, 6 into 72 goes 12 times, and therefore it would take 12 years for your money to double. If you were getting 12%, it would take 6 years for your money to double."

"Ahh, I get it," said David. "So the 18% my credit card company charges me would only take 4 years for the money to double."

"That is exactly right," smiled Zane. "So to explain it again, let's draw out this example. Let's say the average person gets his or her first credit card in university or college and by the age of 24 has two credit cards, each with a balance of about $5,000. That would total $10,000." He leaned back in his chair. "Now, we know that the average person will keep those balances on his or her card until about age 56."

"Really that long?" asked Sarah shocked.

"Yes, that long, and I've run into many people in their 60's who still have credit card debt. That's why the bank calls it 'revolving credit' because most people never fully pay it off on a regular basis."

"I know what you mean," David said sheepishly, "I've had a balance on mine for the last eight years."

Sarah glanced at David in amazement.

"Okay," Zane refereed, "No blaming or victim talk here. Let's just learn and improve."

Zane started drawing the chart below as Sarah and David's eyes grew wider and wider:

Rule of 72 at 18%:   Money doubles every 4 years

Age	24	10,000
	28	20,000
	32	40,000
	36	80,000
	40	160,000
	44	320,000

48	640,000
52	1,280,000
56	2,560,000

"Essentially what this means is that as the credit card companies keep reinvesting the interest you pay them, they can keep increasing their investment. So you see, you and many other people are providing the credit card companies with an opportunity to invest at an 18% rate of return. They're able to turn the $10,000 you borrowed from them into $2,560,000.Their stunned looks when faced with the truth encouraged Zain to continue. "Let me put it another way. Sarah, you are 24 years old now, correct?"

Sarah squirmed a little, "That's right."

"If you had saved $10,000 by age 24 and invested it at 18%, you could retire at 60 with $5,120,000."

David, at a loss for words, could only say, "Wow!"

"Wow is right, David." agreed Zane. "That's the power of compound interest over time. Let me show you another example with these twin brothers. John invested $2,000 per year in a great investment from age 20 to age 30 and then stopped putting money in. His brother Paul decided to do the same from age 30 to age 60. Look at the chart I am going to draw up to see the difference between them when they both retire at age 60."

John:			Paul:	
20	2000		30	2000
30	x10		60	30 years
	20,000 invested			60,000 invested

Zane pulled out his iPhone, found the financial calculator, punched in John's numbers, and came up with 6,744,530 at age 60. Then he punched in Paul's numbers and came up with 1,581,895 at age 60.

"Hard to believe isn't it?" he said. "John only invested 20,000 and he has over five million more than his brother Paul, who invested 40,000 more of his hard earned money. Do you see why time is of the essence?"

"I sure do!" Sarah replied. "They shouldn't allow kids to graduate high school without knowing this stuff."

"You're absolutely right," said Zane.

"Okay, okay, I see it now," exclaimed David, "Now, how do I get rid of the debt, and how can I make 18% on my future investment?"

Zane smiled at David as he loved his get-to-the-bottom-line attitude. "Well David, you already did the first thing, which was to pay yourself first and create an emergency fund. Now, it's time to start Step Two: Pay off all consumer debt."

"Remind me what consumer debt is again?" asked Sarah.

"Good question. It's all debt accumulated through consumerism, that is the purchase of things that you consume. If you put eating out or groceries on your credit card, then it is consumer debt. If you put something that goes down in value on credit, or said another way its value depreciates or is consumed, than that is consumer debt."

"So my car loan is consumer debt?" asked David.

"Exactly," responded Zane. "The only debts that are not consumer debt are loans to buy real estate, businesses or investments, and we'll go over these in detail when we talk about wealth building."

"Is that next?" asked David.

"No, not right now," Zane replied. "We need to eliminate all consumer debt from your life first and forever."

"Forever?" quipped Sarah.

"Yes, forever. Debt for consumer items will become a thing of the past for you and David as you journey along the path of wealth building."

David shook his head amazedly, "Boy have I ever messed things up!"

"Remember," said Zane, "No blame or victim mentality here. We're only going to go forward."

"How long will it take to dig out of the hole I've dug?" David asked.

"Well, it'll take some time, but it may happen faster than you think. Think of it like losing weight. It took time to put the weight on and it will take time and effort to take it back off. Just like weight loss. There are specific ways to lose weight and keep it off, just as there are special ways to make loosing your debt more efficient. Remember I said I had consolidated my debts four times and had gone back into debt?"

The couple nodded.

"This was like the crash diet. I lost debt quickly but did not change my habits so I went further in debt once my financial pain was relieved. Many people try a shotgun approach to getting rid of debt. This means they take any surplus money and divide it among all their debts. The problem with this approach is that you don't see results and can become discouraged quickly. Think of the sun; it's the most powerful thing we know of and yet you can stay under it for hours."

Zane was getting so excited now that his voice started to crack. David hopped up to get him more water. Zane thanked him and leaned in eagerly.

"Okay, now the average person can risk being exposed to strong sunlight for about 20 minutes without getting burnt because the sun's power is spread out over half of the earth and outer space. A laser on the other hand is not a real strong source of power, but it can burn you in seconds because it is so focused. As a matter of fact, when I had laser eye surgery, for correcting my distance sight problem, it only took 24 seconds for one eye and 28 seconds for the second eye to burn through the corneal tissue and trim the lenses into the right shape. Laser focus is the way we are going to eliminate your debt."

"Laser focus," repeated David.

Zane smiled, "Yes laser focus. We're going to put an all out extra focus on your smallest debt and then move on to the next smallest. Let's lay them all out in Sarah's journal with the minimum payment, balance and interest rate."

	Minimum Payment	Balance	Interest Rate
Credit Card 1	250	5,000	18%
Credit Card 2	170	3,000	18%

Electronic Store	0	1,500	28%
Furniture Store	200	2,600	28%
Back Taxes	300	6,000	11%
Sarah's Car	271	3,400	7%
Department Store	90	800	28%
David's car	600	18,000	8%
TOTAL	1881	40,300	

"Ok guys. That's a fair list of debt to pay off. It totals $40, 300."

Upon seeing Sarah tearing up, Zain continued encouragingly, "Believe it or not, Sarah, this amount is still lower then the average family's consumer debt."

Sarah wiped her eyes. "Maybe," she murmured, "It just looks like an insurmountable amount when you put it down on paper."

"Well Sarah," explained Zane, "It's like when you go to a new mall and you want to get to Victoria's Secret. The first place you look at is the map of the mall."

"Yes that's right," Sarah said with a puzzled look as to what in the world Victoria's Secret had to do with the amount of debt they had.

"Stay with me," said Zane. "What is the first thing you look for on the map?"

"That's easy," David blurted out. "The red dot."

"Yes, the red dot," added Sarah.

"Exactly," exclaimed Zane. "The red dot shows you where you are and then you can figure out how to best get to your destination. You see, this chart of debts does the same thing. You can find a blank form on my website www.wealth-formula.com. This chart is the red dot that tells us where we are, and we know that where we want to go is to consumer debt free. Now let's look at the path that will get us there the fastest and with a few milestones along the way. First of all, now that you're paying cash for things you buy and have an emergency fund or a cushion, do you need your credit cards any longer?"

"No!" they both replied.

"Well then, it's time to make an ornament for your window," Zane said.

David and Sarah turned to each other and smiled, as neither one of them had a clue what Zane was talking about, yet they knew that if they trusted him and followed along, things would eventually be cleared up.

Zane broke the silence, "Sarah please turn the oven onto 400°F and bring us a cookie sheet and some baker's paper. David grab a pair of scissors and all of your credit cards."

Sarah and David returned in a few moments with the items.

"Now, cut up all your cards and place the pieces overlapping on the baker's paper on the cookie sheet, and let's put it into the oven for 15 minutes."

"You've got to be kidding!" David gasped.

"Do I look like I'm kidding?" Zane smiled. "No dad jokes here!"

"No," Sarah said as she grabbed the first card and cut it into a six pieces.

Now David was getting into it and he took the scissors out of Sarah's hand and started cutting.

"This is so freeing!" he said as he cut up his credit card. "No longer will this card be the maser of me!" he said as he remembered the sermon from last Sunday, which had said that since the borrower is slave and the lender is master, no wonder they call it 'MasterCard.' He smiled as he chopped the card into pieces. A few minutes later they pulled the melted collage out of the oven and let it cool.

"Now you can put a hole in there, tie a string through it, and hang it in your window as a reminder of where you have come from." explained Zane.

"This is hilarious!" said Sarah. "Let's hang it in the kitchen window so that we can remember when we're washing dishes every day that we're heading to be debt free!"

"I like that," David said.

"Now the fun part is over," Zane piped up. "Let's get down to work on getting rid of this debt forever. Let's put numbers beside them in the order we are going to pay them off. Smallest to largest."

"Okay, can I try?" Sarah jumped in.

"Sure." Zane grinned.

"Okay, so the smallest is the department store, so we would pay that off first and then the electronics store."

"That's right," prompted Zane.

"No, wait!" David blurted out, "That is at zero percent and not due yet!"

"Correct," said Zane, "and yet we want to pay it off before it is due because if we miss the due date by just one day, interest will be added back to the first day that you purchased the item. Additionally, by paying the smallest first, we get to celebrate a win sooner. Also, your payment's size will increase as we pay off each debt. In other words, our laser is getting stronger and stronger."

"Okay," said David, "I guess that makes sense. So then the next one would be the other furniture store and then the second credit card."

"Right. You guys seem to have it down pat," applauded Zane.

"Yes," said Sarah, "though there isn't any extra money in the budget to pay the debt down faster."

Zane smiled, "Let's look at that. David is already working two jobs plus finishing up the house, so he can't do any more, and Sarah you are working part time, correct?"

"Yes that's right," Sarah answered, "and I'm doing school online so that I can become a Real Estate Agent.

"That's fantastic Sarah," Zane said, "One of the things I want to teach you is that any investment you put into yourself to make you a higher income earner, more promotable, or able to run your own business pays dividends for the rest of your life. Good for you!"

David spoke up now, grinning shyly. "Sarah I was waiting to tell you till I heard for sure, but now seems to be a good time. I've been applying at other jobs that pay more and won't have me quite so tired at night, so I should be able to do more around the house in the evenings."

"That would be so good," sighed Sarah.

"You guys are really on the right track now," said Zane. "Here's how to pay off the debt. You know the money you alotted in the budget for the emergency fund?"

Sarah and David nodded.

"Well, since your emergency fund bucket is full, you now have that money available to you, provided you keep the bucket full. Now, every month you will add that available money to your smallest debt to accelerate your debt repayment until any emergency comes up. When this happens, stop the debt repayment acceleration, only pay the minimum, and then build the emergency fund or cushion back up once the emergency has passed. Once your emergency fund is built back up, go back to knocking off the debt. Let's run through this and see how long it will take. Oh yes, before we do that I have another insight for you. Would that be okay?"

"We're game," they replied.

"Great! Let's talk about the Wealth Slippage Principal. David, you know when you want to accelerate as fast as possible in your car that you should not over power at the start or your tires will slip and you will not go as fast."

"Sure, I understand," said David, "And what does that have to do with wealth building?"

"Well, most people let money slip through their fingers in quarters and dollars. They don't track the small amounts and wealth slips through their fingers one coffee, coke, or hamburger at a time."

David started to clue in, "Are you talking about my sixty dollars a month in the budget that I spend on coffee and snacks?"

Zane shook his head, "I was more talking about when people don't keep track, using their debit cards for small purchases, and have no idea where their money went at the end of the month. They end up with the classic case of too much month and not enough money."

"I see," smiled David proudly, thankful that for once Zane mentioned a habit he didn't have.

Zane continued, "Now just for fun, let's put your $60 a month into an RRSP. And let's say you also invest the tax saving, since the sixty dollars you spend is after tax dollars, and an RRSP allows pre-tax dollars to be invested."

"I get it," David said, "This is the pre or after tax lesson from before."

Zane glowed, loving David's application of the earlier lesson. "Exactly." He pulled out his financial calculator. "This means, if you are taxed at 25%, your tax savings will be about $15. So now, your $60 really becomes $75.

"Great. Let's say you put the $75 each month into an RRSP starting from age 28 until age 65 when you plan to retire. That would make you retire with $28,860 of money."

"Wow! That's a lot of Coke and fast food," Sarah reasoned.

"It sure is! Now, here's the really neat part: let's see what it is with *compound* interest." Zane punched a few numbers into his phone and then turned it towards the couple. Both their jaws dropped as they read the number 571,024.

"That's unbelievable!" cried David. "You mean that my Cokes and coffee at only two dollars a day are costing me over half a million dollars?!"

"That's right David," Zane laughed, poking David's mug teasingly. "I hope you really enjoy your half a million dollar coffee!"

Sarah jumped in, "Where can I get that calculator? I have friends that smoke and drink to the tune of about $20 dollars a day, and I'd love to share this information with them."

Zane replied, "If you go to my wealth-formula website, I have a tool where you can enter your age, when you want to retire, what you spend and what you save, and by changing the numbers and the rate of return you can see what your amount will be at your age of retirement. It is a very cool Excel matrix."

"That's great," said Sarah. "I'll log on at work next week and send the link to my friends!"

David's face brightened. "Zane, do you mean if I stop spending some of my 60 dollars temporarily, we can pay the debt off quicker?"

"That sure is a possibility."

David beamed excitedly, "Okay, Sarah, I can live on just $20 a month until we're debt free. After all, I brought most of the debt into our relationship."

This was so much to take in that Sarah was becoming emotional. She explained to Zane how she had been making the daily choice to forgive David and release both of them from guilt and resentment. "I am so glad you said that, David." She leaned over to hug him and ran her fingers through his hair. "You are the love of my life and I wouldn't want anyone else. This debt is not the way I had envisioned starting off my marriage that I dreamed about as a little girl. I wouldn't trade the learning we are getting for anything though!"

"That's a great attitude," said Zane. "Forgiveness will release you from a clench that's a lot tighter and far more damaging than any financial grip." He stretched contentedly. "And now, we need to walk through your debt elimination before I have to go. I have another important date."

"If it's not too personal," Sarah asked, "what is the date you normally have on a Saturday evening?"

"Well," revealed Zane, "I used to be in survival mode like you are, wondering where I would find the money to pay the rent or buy the groceries. Then I started reading every financial book I could find. The first book I read was *The Wealthy Barber,* then I read *The Richest Man in Babylon* and then books like *Financial Peace, The Millionaire Mind, The Millionaire Next Door, Rich Dad Poor Dad, The One Minute Millionaire, Smart Couples Finish Rich, The Automatic Millionaire, Till Debt Do Us Part, Managing God's Money* et cetera. The more I read, the more my life started to change. I found after about ten books, my head knowledge was great and the knowledge started to seep into my heart, which then effected the decisions I made. It wasn't long before success started to follow me everywhere I went. Once I had a lot of wealth piled up, I recognized something."

Sarah was franticly trying to keep up in her journal.

"What was that?" David asked intently.

"Well, it was that my life lacked meaning. I had gone from survival to stability, made it to success, and now it was time to move on to significance. In significance, it's no longer about me but others. I continue to build wealth, except that it's not for me, it's for charity. One of the grass roots organizations I support is You Feed Them. It's an organization that creates agricultural support for communities in Africa, and their goal is to eliminate world hunger one village at a time. You can find more information on their website: www.youfeedthem.com. Now, that's enough about me. Let's get working on the debt elimination plan."

"I'm good with that," said Sarah. "Put me down for $40 as well. I can live with having $20 a month for spending money too. At least until our debt is paid off." She smiled shyly at David.

Zane glanced down at the notebook. "Okay, let's take that $500 per month that was going to the cushion and add it to the $80 you both so generously offered out of the budget. Now you have $580. Now, add that to the $90 you were already paying the department store, and in a month you will pay off $670, so with interest it will take 1½ months to pay off the department store and then it is gone forever."

"Cool!" David exclaimed. He rubbed his hands together wickedly. "And the power of laser focus begins!"

Zane chuckled. "Next, take the other $300 or so that is left over from month two, since you paid off the department store, and pay an extra $250 on the electronic store. Take the left over $50 and you can have dinner or a movie to celebrate your first debt being gone."

"I like that!" sighed Sarah. "Restaurant food!"

Zane continued, "You now owe $1250 on the electronic store and at $580, plus the $90 you were paying the department store, you can put $670 on the electronic store. In the next 2 months, you will have the electronic store paid off and have $90 dollars extra left over that month."

"Wow!" said David, "Our laser is getting intense!"

"Is it ever!" said Zane. "Now, watch this. The power of laser focus becomes incredible. Let's say you put an extra $40 on the the furniture store and then again take the $50 and celebrate. Maybe this time it will be a bottle of wine and steak for dinner or lunch out with friends after church. Now, let's say you have to put snow tires for your car, so you take $1,300 out of the cushion. It will take you two months of the $670 to pay that back to the cushion so you have $2000. After six months the furniture store balance will be somewhere around $2,000. So, you take the $670, add it to the $200 your were paying the furniture store, so now you will be paying $870. This means it will take three months to pay off the furniture store. We are now nine months in, you still have the $2000 cushion *and* you have wiped out three of your debts. How do you feel?

"Amazing!" shouted Sarah gleefully.

"Plus, you should have an extra $50 or so for another date night."

David nodded his head thoughtfully. "You know Zane, giving up my $40 won't be that bad since I'll have three celebrations with Sarah." He shrugged ruefully. "I totally thought I wasn't going be able to spend a penny for the next five years or something." David shook his head at the thought. "I really expected it was going to be horrible!"

"I am glad you feel that way." Zane said. "The key is to remember that these things are temporary. And a choice. Your money is not the master of you. You could decide to pull out the $80 at any point and spend it on something else. The key here is not to adopt a victim mentality; you *have* the money to do those things if you wish. You are simply *choosing* to prioritize what you spend your money on. Don't ever tell yourself 'I can't afford this or that' because you *can* technically afford them. Instead, say 'It's not a priority at the moment.' This reminds you that you are in control, that you are blessed, and that you are choosing to do something far more worthwhile with your money."

"Hey, that's so true!" realized Sarah. "When I go shopping with no money, it's agony! I spend the whole time feeling poor and wishing I could buy everything I see. And yet, when I go to a store with money to spend, I often come home empty handed. It's like when the choice is given to me, I realize I actually don't want those things that much after all."

"Exactly!" said Zane. "Now, you are going to see your laser get even more powerful. Watch this. You now have $870 cash for debt elimination each month. Let's say the car needs a brake job and you use the cushion, so

$870 needs to go back into the cushion this month. We are now at 10 months. Credit card two is next. It used to be 3000, but you have paid for 10 months, so the balance will be about $2,600. You take the $870 plus the $170 you were paying and pay $1,040. In 2 ½ months this credit card is no longer your master. Let's put the other ½ month or approximately $500 against Sarah's car and $50 for a celebration. We are now at 13 months. Sarah's balance is approximately what?"

"Well, let's see," said Sarah, "I started with $3,400 at 7% interest for the 13 months while I was paying it down. That would be about $252 principal. So, if I paid 13 months at $252, that equals $3,286, so the balance would be about $124. And I have not taken into consideration the $500 we had extra to pay on it."

"You're right Sarah," Zane explained. "So, your car will be paid for, and you still have about $376 to put against the credit card that started at $5,000."

"This is unbelievable!" David said, as he sat more forward in his chair and polished off his second cup of now cold coffee.

"I think the caffeine is getting to you," Sarah joked.

"No it's not!" David grinned, "I just like the light at the end of the tunnel. And for once it's not a train coming at me!"

All three burst out laughing.

"Now, the first credit card balance should be about $3,000. Let's take the $1,040, plus Sarah's car payment of $271, plus the $250 we were paying on the credit card, and we have $1,561 per month so the $3000 balance will be paid off in two months. Let's say David's car needs service to a tune of $1500, so another month is used to top up the emergency cushion. We are now at 16 months and we still have an emergency fund of $2000 and have six of your eight debts totally paid off! Let's look at the back taxes next. After 16 months the new balance would be almost $2,200, and we have $1561 plus the 300 we were paying, so we have $1861 to put towards the taxes each month. $2200 will only take a month and a ¼ to pay off, and we will have about $1500 extra to put down on your last debt, David's car. So, David's car after 16 months will have a balance of about $9,000 minus the $1500 extra you paid for a balance of $7,500."

David spoke up, "Can I finish this one?"

Zane nodded his approval.

David grabbed Sarah's journal and said, "We now have $1861, plus the 600 I was paying. That makes $2461, so it will take just over three months to pay off my car."

"You're right," Zane said. "With interest on the $7,500, it'll take just about an extra $400 in the forth month to pay off your car. Let's say you had a $2,000 emergency to finish up the month. We now have paid off all your debt in 22 months, and you have covered over $5,000 in emergency expenses, and you still have $2,000 in your emergency fund."

David jumped out of his chair, "This is fantastic! In less than two years we'll be debt free!" David grabbed Sarah's hand and pulled her up out of her chair and started dancing around in circles with her singing all the while, "In less than two years we're debt free…In less than two years we're debt free!"

Zane got up out of his chair and said, "Looks like you guys have some celebrating to do. I'm off to my important date."

Sarah smiled, "Oh yeah, you never did tell us what your date was."

Zane smiled broadly. "I coach a teen girls' soccer team."

"Do you get paid to coach?" David asked.

"No," Zane replied, "it's just another way I've found to give back and it makes me feel so alive to help out."

The three said their goodbyes, and David and Sarah waved as the Maserati disappeared into the distance.

Sarah and David went to bed that night with the plan circulating through their minds. It felt like a thousand pounds had been lifted off their shoulders.

<u>Saturday</u>

Ran into Zane at the Brinston corner store. He was buying pizza, so we went home and had lunch together.

    His Advice:
- Wealth account is never to be spent, only invested. It's our legacy account
- The highest return we can get right now is paying off consumer debt
- The rule of 72 — divide the rate of return into 72 and the answer is roughly how many years it would take to double your investment
- Since Visa is collecting 18%, that goes into 72 four times, so it would take Visa 4 years to double their $10,000 investment through someone's consumerism

CREDIT CARD INCREASE:

AGE	18% RETURN
24	10,000
28	20,000
32	40,000
36	80,000
40	160,000
44	320,000
48	640,000
52	1,280,000

OUR LASER FOCUS:

	MINIMUM PAYMENT	TOTAL OWING	PERCENT INTEREST
6 Credit card #1	250	5000	18%
4 Credit card #2	170	3000	18%
2 Electronic store	0	1500	28%
3 Furniture store	200	2600	28%
7 Back taxes	300	6,000	11%
5 Sarah's car	271	3,400	7%
1 Department store	90	800	28%
David's car	600	18,000	8%
	1881	40,300	

- Pay the smallest loans first and start increasing the debt pay down by adding the paid off loan payments to the next smallest debt
- Other books to consider reading:

☐ **The Wealthy Barber** – David Chilton

- [ ] ***The Richest Man in Babylon*** – George Clason
- [ ] ***Financial Peace*** – Dave Ramsey
- [ ] ***The Millionaire Mind*** – T. Harv Eker
- [ ] ***The Millionaire Next Door*** – Thomas J. Stanley and William D. Danko
- [ ] ***Rich Dad Poor Dad*** – Robert T. Kiyosaki
- [ ] ***The One Minute Millionaire*** – Mark Victor Hansen and Robert G. Allen
- [ ] ***Smart Couples Finish Rich*** – David Bach
- [ ] ***The Automatic Millionaire*** – David Bach
- [ ] ***Till Debt Do Us Part*** – Julie Ann Barnhill
- [ ] ***Managing God's Money*** – Michel A. Bell

Survival » Stability » Success » Significance

With the laser focus plan, we can be debt free in less than TWO YEARS!!! What a relief it is to have a plan to eliminate our debt. I will sleep well tonight!

MY DECISIONS AND ACTION ITEMS.

Fill out the debt elimination form on www.wealth-formula.com

Decide what I can give up to accelerate my laser focus on debt elimination.

How many months to pay off all consumer debt?

Show my plan to someone for accountability.

Which book on Finances am I going to read next?

Am I in Survival, Stability, Success, or Significance as per Zane's definition?

RIDING IT OUT...THIRD GEAR

David and Sarah awoke the next day with a new attitude, a challenge ahead of them, and a plan in hand to get it accomplished.

David made his lunch and filled up a couple of water bottles and a thermos of freshly brewed Tim Horton's coffee. Sarah had found Tim Horton's ground coffee at the grocery store and bought it fresh. "Have a great day," Sarah said as she kissed him goodbye and went back inside to continue to study for her first of three real estate exams that was coming up in three weeks.

Weeks went by and every Saturday David and Sarah went for a long bike ride. David secretly hoped that they would run into Zane on their trips. Sarah suspected this was partly because David had never met anyone like him before and didn't have many close male friends to share his aspirations and trials with. Though David may not have realized this need himself, for his part he was aware of how thankful he was to have Sarah. She was such a sweet caring person who always looked out for others, including himself. That's why she was so suited to serving people in real estate. He was really proud of her when she passed her first exam; whenever he saw her taking the time to say hello to neighbours, he knew she was going to be a great REALTOR® because she cared so much for people.

Time flew by and before Sarah realized it, they were going on their sixth bike ride since Zane had spent that long afternoon with them laying out a plan. Friday night had been a particularly special date night as David arrived from work with his arms loaded and a boyish grin. He had brought a bottle of strawberry wine, the same kind they had at their wedding, and a couple of fillet minion steaks. David proudly held up the bottle of wine and shouted with joy. "It's time to celebrate! We knocked off the first debt. The department store credit is gone!"

Sarah jumped for joy, unsure of whether it was because she loved a good steak or because they had paid off the first of eight. Frankly, she didn't care. She felt great.

It was now Saturday and she was excited to go for their weekly bike ride. Sarah had woken up early and put together a picnic lunch. There was potato salad she had made from the left over potatoes of Friday's celebration, breaded chicken left over from the Thursday night meal she had made, some celery and carrot sticks, a bag of chips, and of course a few cans of Coke. After she packed it all in the checkered little basket set they received as a wedding present, she heard rumbling upstairs. As David came down the stairway, she flashed him a wide smile and asked him what he would like to do today.

"I would love to go for a bike ride," David said ruffling his hair sleepily, "but I have a ton of things to do around here."

"Like what?" she asked.

David pulled out the list he had written upstairs. "I need to cut the grass, paint the wood around the windows in the loft area, paint the garage door, fix the steps to the front door with new cement, weed the garden, and do a load of laundry so I'll have work clothes for Monday. I understand we are going to your parents after church Sunday, so I need to finish it all up today."

"That's okay." Sarah said hiding her disappointment, "It's good for you to have your Sunday as a day of rest. Let's have some toast for a quick breakfast, and I'll help you get the chore list done. Then maybe we can go out on our speedy bicycle built for two!"

"Sounds good to me," David replied.

David started the lawn mower as Sarah threw in the first load of laundry.

When David rounded the corner with the mower, he was surprised to see Sarah up on a ladder painting the window frames. He knew she was afraid of any height higher than a chair.

The couple worked all morning and right through to the afternoon. When the list was complete, David said, "Let's have a quick shower and then we can go."

"Do you realize it's already four o'clock?" Sarah asked.

"No," said David. "Where has the day gone? I wondered why I was so hungry."

"Grab your shower, and I'll put some food on the table," suggested Sarah.

David came down to a feast of chicken, veggies, and potato salad. "Wow! When did you have time to get all this ready?" he asked.

Sarah explained it was to be a picnic lunch she had prepared early this morning.

"Aww, sorry for ruining your plans," apologized David.

"That's okay," Sarah replied. "We needed those things to be done for awhile, so it was good to do it while you had the energy. Not many women would complain about their husband doing work around the house," she smiled pleasantly. "And anyways, we can still go for a ride after we eat."

The couple wolfed down their food, tidied up, and jumped on the bike.

"Where do you want to go?" asked David.

"Where no man has gone before!" declared Sarah dramatically.

"West is probably best then," David suggested sensibly.

"Sure," agreed Sarah. They headed out of the driveway.

They had peddled for about an hour when they came to the small town of Kemptville. "Bathroom break!" Sarah called, poking David in the back good naturedly.

They headed over to the park since there were outhouses by the soccer fields that she could use. As they approached the enclosure, David was the first to notice the familiar sports car. "Look!" he pointed, "I think that's Zane's Maserati in the parking area!"

After Sarah rushed back from the bathroom, they headed off for a walk around the fields to see if they could find Zane. It didn't take long as they soon heard Zane yelling encouraging instructions to his team at the top of his lungs. David and Sarah found a good spot to sit down and watched the play.

At half time, Sarah called out to one of the girls and asked what the score was. She told Sarah it was one to zero for Kemptville over Ottawa. Zane hadn't noticed the couple as he was so focused on coaching the girls. The girls quickly got a drink of water and then quietly huddled around Zane so they could hear every word he had to say. Sarah and David strained to hear what Zane said but he spoke too quietly.

The whistle for the start of the second half broke the silence, and then the girls from Ottawa got in a small huddle for a cheer and ran onto the pitch. Sarah and David couldn't help marveling how they played like a changed team. They ran faster on the ball, communicated with their teammates more, passed the ball in short tight passes, and were spread out on the field. One outside left passed the ball to a midfield who saw the outside left making a sprint for the goal. A quick give and go pass back to the outside left player and she was running hard down the wing. The defense was pulling over to try to cover her. At just the perfect moment, she crossed the ball towards the far post, and one of the forwards headed the ball into the net. The goalie didn't have a chance.

David and Sarah looked at each other amazedly and said, "That was a great play!"

The play went on for a while back and forth down the field with the score tied at one. The ball headed back towards the Kemptville end when the forward called for a through ball. The midfielder immediately chipped the ball over the defense's head just far enough for the forwards to sprint through and not two hard that the goalie could come out. The forward ran in on the goalie, faked a shot to the left, pulled the ball right, and gently popped the ball into the net as the goalie had gone left.

"Wow! What a beautiful goal," Sarah exclaimed.

"Sure was," David replied.

The two teams lined up and it wasn't long before Ottawa scored another goal by passing their way up the field. The ball ended up in the right corner, and the goalie was playing a little out of her net expecting a pass. The right winger noticed the position of the keeper and lofted a ball over the keeper's head that dropped in just below the crossbar.

"What a perfectly placed shot," Sarah commented. She had played soccer in junior high and high school and knew a great game when she saw one.

The referee blew the whistle for the end of the match. The Ottawa team ran back to congratulate their keeper and then lined up with Zane at the end of the line to shake the hands of the opposition and congratulate them on a well fought game.

After jogging over to gather his things, Zane noticed David and Sarah. He grinned as he grabbed a stray soccer ball and dropped it back into a mesh net bag. "I thought I might be seeing you soon."

After the teams cleared the fields and went home, the three friends sat on the grass and Sarah asked Zane what he had said at half time to totally change the way the girls played the second half.

"Well it was quite simple," Zane explained. "I told them they were better than what they had been playing. I said forget the first half, it's a new game and we need to beat the opposition by at least two goals in this new game. They realized that they needed to dig deep and play hard to beat a team by two goals in a half game. Next, I told them to remember what we practiced and to work as a team. Individually they were all skilled players, but individually they could not beat this opposition of eleven players. They needed to work as a team to divide and conquer the opposition and to focus on their play, not to worry or react to anything that opposition might do."

"Well it sure worked," Sarah stated. "Your team was a cool cucumber out there the second half and executed those set plays beautifully."

"I know," said Zane, "I'm really proud of them."

David broke in "I think you will be proud of us as well."

"Really?" asked Zane.

"Yeah!" David beamed. "We paid off our first debt, had a celebration last night, and it feels great!"

"That's wonderful," Zane said. "Everyone needs a win from time to time."

"It sure did feel good to be filling in the debt hole we've dug instead of digging in deeper.", David Chirped.

"I am so proud of you and how far you have come in such a short time.", replied Zane.

"Hey," David said, "look's like you're our financial coach."

"You're right," Zane replied. "It's very important that people have coaches or mentors in the important areas of life and pay for expert wisdom when needed." He leaned back against a tree and rolled his ankles comfortably. "Two areas we haven't talked about yet are wills and insurance."

"Wills and insurance?" questioned David. "Why do we need to worry about that? We're both young and healthy."

"Exactly," Zane said, "so why not take care of it now so that if something unexpected happens, you're prepared? I call this being prepared for the unexpected."

"Huh," Sarah murmured.

Zane continued,"We know that unexpected things happen to people all the time right?"

"Right."

"Well, if they happen all the time, they're not really unexpected. Take your cushion for example; when your furnace broke down unexpectedly, you had the money to pay for the repair in cash. That means you were ready for the unexpected."

"I see," said David.

Zane continued again, "A will is the same sort of thing. You can get a will done professionally by a lawyer for about $500. You'll each want one. Lawyers can write them to include future children or grandchildren so that you don't have to change them very often, if at all. At the same time, your lawyer should prepare a living will and a power of attorney for each other you. Giving power of attorney to your spouse means he or she has the right to sign on your behalf in matters of property. The living will on the other hand states your desires if you are incapable of making medical decisions and gives signing authority for your spouse to make medical decisions on your behalf."

Sarah's brow wrinkled. "But we're so young; it's morbid to talk about these things."

"I know," said Zane, "and yet I am sure you don't want the government deciding your fate or where your children will go if something happens to you. Unfortunately, I know a couple that died in a car accident at thirty and they left a five and seven year old behind with no insurance money or directions as to who was to look after them."

"That's terrible," Sarah answered. "I can make an appointment with our lawyers first thing next week."

"Perfect," said Zane. "The next thing I would like to discuss is life insurance. Most people have too little or no insurance, and many others buy the wrong type. I would strongly suggest you do not purchase the kind of life insurance that has any sort of saving component, cash value, or repayment of premiums if you don't use it. All of these are too expensive."

"Really?" asked Sarah. "I thought it might be a great way to save. This way it's all bundled into one and is easier to manage."

"Understandable," continued Zane, "however, there is an old saying: 'Buy term insurance and invest the rest.' You can out perform that savings part of insurance elsewhere. Another type of insurance I would never buy is mortgage insurance unless you don't qualify medically for term insurance and don't require to medically qualifying for the mortgage insurance. The problem with mortgage or any other loan life insurance is that: one, it is typically more expensive than term; and two, the amount of insurance coverage you have decreases as your mortgage or loan is paid down over the years."

Sarah flicked an ant off her elbow and rested her chin on her knees, pen quickly filling her notebook pages. "Zane, how much insurance should we have? I am always afraid to talk to insurance sales people as I think they normally try to over sell."

"Not so," said Zane. "They may try to sell products that are more expensive or poor investments, but since most people are underinsured, they can't be over selling term insurance. As far as how much is required, it's a peace of mind thing. There is a general guideline that says you should each have 10 times the highest income earner's gross salary."

"Really?" David asked. "Why ten times?"

"Well, let's say you make $50,000 per year and God forbid, something happens to you. For Sarah to be financially okay, would it make sense that your insurance should replace the $50,000 per year that you presently make?"

"Yeah that makes sense," David replied.

Zane explained, "To replace an income it takes investments of 10 times. So a $500,000 investment at 10% rate of return would give you $50,000 per year of income."

"Okay," nodded David, "I see why $500,000 insurance for me, but since Sarah doesn't make that much money, why should we have $500,000 insurance on her as well?"

Zane nodded in understanding. "It's because usually the person earning less is working less and does more at home, or may even stay at home and look after the kids. It would cost a lot of money to replace that person if you still needed to go to work each day. The second reason is if something happened to both of you, there is usually twice as much that would be required to support your children until they can support themselves."

Zain glanced up at the fading sun. "It's getting late and I know you need to start your bike ride home, but there are four more important things you should know about term insurance. First of all, the longer the term, usually the higher the monthly premium because it remains the same for the whole term and you are getting older, so thus more risk of dying at the end. Second, make sure that it is guaranteed renewable at the end of the term in case you have gotten sick and could not get new insurance. Third, don't pay extra for the insurance to increase if it's an accidental death. No matter how one dies, the survivors need the same amount of benefits. Fourth, some companies have term insurance available when you work there; make sure you can keep it if you leave the company, and if not, take what the company you work for gives for free as a bonus, and source your own term insurance for the full amount you need somewhere else so you can keep it if you change jobs."

"One more thing," said Zane. "As you get older and have no dependents, larger assets and no debt, the requirement for life insurance diminishes. That means if you have no children living at home, no debt on your house or anything else, and a million invested, you really don't need insurance because you are self insured."

"Thanks a lot!" Sarah and David said at the same time. "You really have simplified the insurance process for us."

"You're welcome," said Zane. "Just before I go, there are two other types of insurance you may want to investigate."

"What are those?" Sarah inquired as she reopened her journal.

"The first is critical illness, which is a relatively new product. If you get one of the listed diseases, you automatically receive the face amount of the insurance so that you can take some time off and get excellent medical care, without having to worry about money on top of being sick. The second one is long term disability. This insurance can be fairly expensive, but it can be a little less if you increase the length of waiting time from being disabled until benefits are paid. Also, there is disability insurance that pays as long as you cannot perform your original type of work and others that pay only until you can do some other type of work. As you have more of a financial cushion in the future, it will allow a longer waiting period on disability insurance because you will have money to use while you wait. Oh and one more thing… if the disability insurance is paid by your employer then the claim will be taxable and if you pay for the insurance with after tax dollars yourself the disability money will be tax free."

David stood up and shook the grass off his clothes. "Thanks a lot Zane. You sure are giving us lots to consider."

"You've opened our eyes to a lot of things we'd never considered before," agreed Sarah.

The couple said their goodbyes, gave their congratulations on a well coached game, and headed back towards Brinston. There was a cold chill in the air as they headed home, so they peddled as quickly as possible.

As fall approached, daylight hours became shorter and shorter so there was often little light for cycling when David got home, but on warm Saturdays David would pull out the bike and off they would go, hoping to run into Zane. After about a month with no sign of Zane and already the first snowfall of the season, David disappointedly hung the red bike from a rafter in the garage.

He received a phone call while at work on the Monday from Coke asking him to come in for an interview. He didn't tell Sarah as he wanted to surprise her if he got the job.

A week later he got the call; he had received a job offer. When David arrived home that night he waltzed in with a case of Coke in his hands.

"Hi Sarah," he said and gave her a big hug and kiss. "Do you know why I have a case of Coke in my hands?" he asked Sarah with a playful nudge.

Sarah nudged him back, "Because you blew the budget and bought one?"

"Well I guess you're right," said David. "And because I got the job at Coke I wanted and start in two weeks."

"That's awesome!" screamed Sarah in excitement. She was hoping that David wouldn't have to spend another winter picking up garbage.

David explained he would be getting a pay increase of $3 an hour.

"I'm so glad!" exclaimed Sarah.

That Sunday David and Sarah planned to have lunch with Sarah's parents after church. Ruth had pulled out a pot roast and placed it in a slow cooker with potatoes and carrots before church, and by the time they arrived, the kitchen was filled with the smell of black pepper seasoning. Sarah chatted with her mother about her week as she helped mix a jug of juice, while David and Michael talked about David's new job with Coke.

After a lively discussion over lunch of David relaying all the bad experiences at work the previous year, including the sour milk episode, everyone had laughed a great deal and were in a good mood. David shook his head and leaned back in his chair, smiling to himself. Sarah then began to share how well they were doing on paying off their debt.

"It's strange," explained David as he stretched out to pat his stomach, "this budget thing is starting to feel second nature. At first I found it really hard, but now..." his voice trailed off.

"You know," said Ruth, getting up to start the coffee machine, "when you stop thinking of all the things a budget prevents you from doing, and focus instead on the opportunities a budget actually gives you, it's amazing how quickly your priorities change."

"I agree," said Sarah. "The peace of mind we have now is worth so much more than the clothes I used to buy and all the other things I thought we needed."

"I bet you don't go window shopping much anymore either," her mother commented, pulling mugs out of the dishwasher.

"I don't, actually," said Sarah. "Even if I go to just look around, I fall back into that trap and get tempted all over again."

"It's amazing how little people actually need to be happy. The problem begins when we start focusing on what we want rather than on what we have." Ruth reminded.

"Life is definitely more peaceful," Sarah agreed. She pulled the tea bag out of her mug and added milk. "It feels like we are much more in control of our life." One more month she explained and the electronic store would be paid off. She also explained the plan Zane had laid out to pay things off with laser focus. "I wish we could talk with Zane as now we have about $400 extra each month, and it would be good to know what to do with it."

Ruth suggested they look at the budget together and the debt repayment plan to see if they could give some suggestions. As the couples poured over the budget, Ruth asked, "What are the percentages beside giving/tithing, saving, and wealth building?"

"Those are goals to work towards attaining," David explained.

Ruth rubbed her neck and passed the paper back to him. "Why not put some in those categories and the rest in more debt repayment acceleration?"

"I like the sound of that," Sarah said.

On the way home David and Sarah discussed where and how much to apply the blessing of the higher income they had received.

"Why don't we put $100 towards tithing," said David, "build wealth with $200, and pay an extra $100 per month on debt?"

"That sounds good to me," Sarah said. "The new income is an unexpected blessing and it makes sense to move towards our goal of tithing 10% to the church. I'm also excited about paying our debts off faster. Once they're gone, it'll be a wonderful thing to have the luxury to give to those less fortunate through charities like Compassion or You Feed Them."

"Sure would," agreed David.

When David got his last payment from the garbage collection job, he was surprised to find that it was $1,000 more than what he expected. He checked his pay stub for a mistake and discovered he had holiday pay and that is where the extra money came from. David showed Sarah the extra money and she said, "You know we can take the extra money and pay off the electronic store, and then we'll be two months ahead of our schedule."

"Works for me," David replied.

David and Sarah continued to put $670 plus the $100 extra against the furniture store. A few months went by and Sarah and David wondered when they would see their friend Zane again. The daylight began to last longer and longer. Sarah anticipated spring coming as she was interested in starting a small garden. She wrote her second real estate exam and came home on a Saturday afternoon feeling on top of the world.

As she pulled out of the parking lot, her car moved much slower than normal; the revolutions of the tachometer were high, and the speed of the car was slow. A phone call to David later, she knew the clutch was slipping. Sarah sighed with relief as she thought back to a few short months ago when a car breakdown not only would have been a car emergency, but a financial emergency as well. Now she knew they had the estimated $1,000 to repair her car in the bank. This would only set their plans behind a couple of months. As Sarah was discussing this with David, he reminded her, "We had calculated some emergencies into the debt repayment plan so we're still on schedule."

"Wow, I feel better now," Sarah announced.

Weeks went by uneventfully, and then David came home grinning again like the cat that swallowed the canary.

"What's up?" Sarah asked as she knew that look.

"What?" David deflected innocently.

"You know," said Sarah. "You have that look again."

"What look?"

"The look like you just bought a new car or something."

David smiled, "Oh, it's much bigger than that."

"Really?" Sarah asked cautiously, "Did you just buy an SUV?" She knew the days of these unfortunate surprises were over, but her stomach gave an uncomfortable flip anyways. She didn't meet David's eye just in case he sensed her doubts.

"No silly," David replied pulling her into a tight hug. He could sense what she was thinking and realized he couldn't blame her. Instead, he chose to be glad Sarah didn't snap in panic the way she used to, now that he no longer gave her reason to, that is. "You know I won't spend any money that is not in the budget. Not anymore."

"Yes, I know," Sarah admitted in relief. "What is it?"

David pulled her onto his lap and rubbed her back. "You know that $200 a month I have been having taken off my pay cheques for Registered Retirement Savings Plan?"

Sarah nodded.

"I just found out that Coke has a plan where they match our contribution by 40%, so every time we put in $200, they put in $80."

"Seriously? That's great!" said Sarah with surprise.

"I know, eh?" David replied, "Where else could we get an instant 40% rate of return on our investment? No where that I'm familiar with."

Another couple of months went by and spring was finally in the air. David pulled down the bike built for two, dusted it off, oiled the chain, filled the tires, and put it outside so that Sarah would see it when she came out.

"You want to go for a ride, do ya?" Sarah grinned when she saw the bike all polished up and ready to go.

"Sure do!" David smiled wickedly. "Let's go Maserati hunting."

David and Sarah headed west towards Kemptville, hoping to find Zane at the park. They didn't see him or the Maserati. In disappointment, they arrived home three hours later.

The next day Sarah and David could barely walk as that was a long trip to take for the first ride of the season. As David stretched out on their bed in his boxer shorts and closed his eyes, Sarah wandered into the room.

"Sore?" she asked.

"Gosh, yes," groaned David good-naturedly. "I pulled muscles I didn't even know I had."

A cold sensation on his legs hit him like a brick wall. He jumped up, startled, and opened his eyes. Sarah laughed as he picked up a handful of ice cubes and dangled them in the air in shock.

"You!" he spluttered.

Sarah yowled in surprise when like lightning he jumped off the bed and grabbed her. "Don't! Don't!" she squealed helplessly as he stuffed the ice cubes down the front of her jeans.

"Don't what?" he asked casually keeping her pinned in front of him. "Don't put ice cubes on your legs? You don't like that?"

"No!" Sarah yelled, trying desperately to shake the blocks down her thighs and onto the floor. "It's freezing!"

David laughed and let her go. Sarah pulled down her pants to pick out the ice cubes, exposing her red legs, and threw one at her husband's head. David chuckled and dodged it easily.

"You're lucky I played soccer in high school, not rugby!" she declared indignantly.

David grinned again and tackled her.

Another week went by, and on Friday David surprised Sarah with a dozen long stemmed roses.

"Oh, David! What are these for?" Sarah exclaimed as she opened the box.

"These are because I love you and it was time to celebrate."

"What do you mean?" Sarah asked. "You know this kind of thing isn't a priority right now."

"Yes, it is," said David. "We paid off the furniture store this week so it was time to celebrate."

"Aww, that's so sweet!" Sarah said as she embraced him, "I love them, but what about a celebration for you?"

David kissed the top of her head. "The look on your face was celebration enough for me. Besides maybe we can celebrate when we go to bed tonight, and that doesn't cost any money."

"I think we can arrange something," Sarah said as she winked at her husband, the ice cube episode still fresh in both their minds. "Maybe I can even pull some ice cubes out of the freezer," she joked.

David laughed and headed upstairs to change.

"And tomorrow," she continued, "can we go for a ride? I just have this good feeling that we may run into Zane."

David paused on the steps and nodded, "For sure."

Saturday morning came, and Sarah could hear whistling in the kitchen. 'That's weird,' she thought. 'David up early on a day he doesn't have to work?'

As Sarah wandered into the room, she saw a full breakfast of scrambled eggs, bacon, and toast almost ready, and the picnic basket was out and packed. "Holy!" she declared, "You have been an early bird this morning, haven't you?"

"I sure have," David greeted her. "You know, I'm starting to feel lighter and lighter as the load of all this debt is coming off my shoulders."

"Me too, hon. Me too," Sarah replied.

After breakfast, they mounted the bike and decided to drive east this time. After two hours David signaled to Sarah to pull over. They both took a long sip out of their water bottles. "We'd better turn back, Sarah," David said. "Do you remember how stiff we were after last week?"

"You're right," said Sarah. "I was just hoping that we would run into Zane before we headed back. I was so convinced we'd see him today." She shook her head dejectedly.

"Me too," replied David.

That night, the lack of a TV a definite influence on their leisure activities, Sarah and David enjoyed a potluck games night with friends. Over the past few months, David had decided potlucks were a much better option than eating out since everyone brought different food and it was like a buffet, except only better since everything was homemade and free.

After everyone left and the couple stood by the sink washing dishes, Sarah mused to David, "Do you think we're not ready for the teacher to appear?"

"You know, I was wondering the same thing. I don't know," replied David. "I thought we were on schedule, but maybe we're missing something. Why don't you pull out your journal and we can review your notes."

"That's a great idea," said Sarah as she dried her hands to get the journal off the coffee table. As she walked back, she read over her notes. "I think I may have found it, David."

"What's that?" David asked.

"Remember last fall at the soccer field?" Sarah continued before David could answer. "We were to get wills done up and also we were to look into life insurance."

"That's right," recalled David. "How did we forget that? I think this constitutes an emergency. We can call on Monday to book an appointment with the lawyer and take the money out of the cushion as we'll have the money to repay it in a week."

"Sounds fine to me," replied Sarah. "Also, I am going to call my mom and dad right now to get the name of their insurance agent, so we can start investigating the life insurance."

"That's a great idea," agreed David.

By Friday, David and Sarah had purchased $500,000 of life insurance each and were just waiting for the medical test from the nurse who was coming to take their blood pressure and a blood sample. Monday was their appointment with the lawyer to have their will drawn up.

"Do you want to go out on a bike ride this Saturday?" Sarah asked calmly from the doctor's bench where the nurse was rolling up her sleeve and swabbing her arm with alcohol.

"You bet," said David, squeamishly turning away. "Let's go down to the St. Lawrence River and have a picnic in the park again."

"David? You're looking a little white," Sarah grinned teasingly.

David put his hands on his hips and took a deep breath. The sight of needles and blood made him feel faint. "I'm just giving you some privacy," he grumbled.

The nurse called David over to the bench next.

Sarah laughed and patted him on the back. "Don't worry," she smiled. "It doesn't actually hurt very much. At least, it won't for a big tough guy like you!"

David laughed and then winced from the needle prick. "Let's just get through this so we can get back on that bike."

Saturday morning came as usual, and David started early to cut the grass so they would have time to make it down to the park for lunch. As they climbed on the bike and rounded the corner, both were hopeful that they would see the Maserati at the corner store, but no such luck. As they picnicked by the water, David kept listening and looking towards the parking lot hoping to see or hear their friend. After a good lunch, they packed up their blanket and basket and got on the bike for the ride home. Both were quiet on the ride back as there was slight disappointment in their moods after not seeing Zane. Monday came quickly, and so did their appointment with the lawyer. Within an hour, Sarah and David were driving home.

"I can't believe how easy and painless that was!" David exclaimed to Sarah.

"You know, you're right," she replied. "I don't know why so many people put this process off. It feels so great to know that if either one of us dies, the other will be looked after. The will even takes into account when we have children and everything so we don't have to redo this as our life situation changes. It just makes me feel so prepared for bringing someone into this world. This was the best $500 we've spent since we got married."

David nodded in agreement. He had been thinking of asking Sarah if she would be interested in trying for a baby. Not totally sure if he was ready himself, David left the question to rest for the time being.

The following Saturday, David woke up to the sound of lawn mowers and chirping birds. He stretched lazily and reached over to give his wife a good morning kiss.

Sarah lay with her face burrowed in a pillow. "How'd you sleep?" she mumbled.

"Like a rock," sighed David contentedly. "Go ahead and sleep in, honey. I've got a lot of things I want to get done around the house today."

Sarah shook her head as she wrapped herself around him and rested her chin on his shoulder. "I've got a ton I want to do too. Let's make a list and see how many we can knock off today."

"Sounds like a plan," replied David. He stroked her hair nonchalantly and then a wicked smile crept onto his face. He grabbed Sarah and lifted her up into the air as she shrieked. "I've got an idea!" he said. "First person to fall off the bed has to make breakfast!"

After cutting the grass, David decided to change the oil in the car. He had drained the oil and was changing the filter when he noticed he only had three liters of synthetic oil. He called over to Sarah who was gardening in the front, "Feel like driving into Kemptville for me? I need some more oil. Just make sure it's the purple synthetic oil though as it's all I'll put in my car. I think Canadian Tire carries it."

Sarah looked a little confused, "David, why don't we both go in to town on the bike? It'll save the cost of gas and I could use a break."

David thought for a moment and then nodded. "I wanted to keep working, but it'll probably do me some good to take a break. Let's take knapsacks and we can pick up a few groceries while we're there."

"Makes sense," Sarah said as she straightened up and rubbed the dirt off her knees.

When the couple arrived at the Canadian Tire, low and behold parked out front by the chip wagon was a Maserati. The couple rode over to the chip truck with great anticipation. As they got closer, they noticed Zane standing in line to order.

Sarah and David blurted out in unison, "Hi Zane!"

"Oh, hi!" said Zane. "I thought I might see you out here today. I'm just about to order a poutine. Would you like one?"

"We sure would," David and Sarah said at the same time. As the couple looked at each other, they shrugged and said, "Fools seldom differ."

Zane piped up, "I prefer to say great minds think alike."

"You're right," said David. "That's much more positive and uplifting."

"Yes," explained Zane, "I find that my attitude has so much to do with my success in life."

Sarah spoke up, "You mean having a positive attitude helped you succeed?"

"Well yes," said Zane, "and yet, I don't have a positive attitude, I have a 'Yes!' attitude."

The couple gave him a puzzled look. "It's like this," explained Zane. "Put your arm up, and then pull it down quickly bending at the elbow, and say with all your enthusiasm, 'Positive!'"

After Sarah did the motion, she felt a little silly as they were still in the line.

Zane asked, "Did you feel a difference in your energy?"

"A little," Sarah admitted.

Zane continued, "Now I want you to do the same thing but with a 'Yes!' attitude. This time when you bring your arm down quickly, I want you to loudly say 'Yesssss!'"

As Sarah and David did as they were told, their faces lit up slightly.

"You're right," said Sarah surprisedly. "That actually makes me feel more energized."

"Me too," said David. "I do feel a bit like a cheesy super hero though," he laughed. "I can imagine if you do that several times a day, you'll feel better about life."

"This good energy has the power to attract great things, just like negative thoughts or energy can bring the wrong results. Some people call this the Law of Attraction. I prefer to refer to a much more ancient concept from the Bible that says 'You reap what you sow'."

"Sewing?" asked David. "Like a dress or something?"

Zane chuckled. "No, sow as in a farmer sows his crops. If you're positive, it's more likely that positive things will be attracted into your life."

As they reached the chip truck, Zane ordered three large poutines and iced teas. Sarah couldn't resist a quick bite of her fries. The gravy was thick and the cheese was so warm and gooey. "Nothing better on a summer's evening than a big bucket of poutine!" she sighed happily.

As the three were walking over to the picnic table, Zane noticed a penny on the ground. He bent down to pick it up, raised his arm, and excitedly declared, "Yes! I am a money magnet." He then put the penny in his pocket.

David looked at him in amazement, "How can someone with so much money get so excited about a penny?" he asked.

"Many people wouldn't bother to bend down for a penny," Zane explained to David. "My attitude and awareness is open to money flowing into my life. This makes me aware of deals and opportunities. There is a part in the brain called the reticular activator that makes the brain aware and alert for certain things."

"I'm not sure I understand," David said.

Zane continued, "Well, think of when you bought your new car. You probably thought it was so unique, and then as soon as you bought it you saw them everywhere and every day."

"You know, you're right," replied David.

"I know," said Zane. "Your reticular activator is turned on for that particular car. It is the same way with money and wealth. What you think about, you talk about, and what you talk about, you bring about."

"I see," said Sarah and David as the three shooed a few birds off the picnic bench and sat down to enjoy their lunch.

The couple filled Zane in on the change of job, paying off their debts so far, and putting some money into savings and giving. "That is fantastic progress," Zane announced. "It was wise to put some funds into savings since Coke was matching it at 40%. Stay on course until all your consumer debt is completely gone, and then you will increase the savings with Coke to the maximum they will match and increase your giving up to the 10% point. When you get there, I'll explain more of what to do with your newfound cash flow."

"That'll be great," said Sarah. "I've been sharing some of what we're learning and doing with some friends. They think I'm crazy and that everyone lives with debt. It's how they maintain their lifestyle."

"Remember what I said about the teacher always being there and the student not being ready to see him or her?"

"Yes," answered Sarah.

"Well, your friends aren't ready to learn." Zane continued, "One of my favourite sayings is: 'A person convinced against his will is of the same opinion still.' When people see the difference in your life, some may ask about the changes. These friends will most likely be ready to hear what you have to say."

"Oh, I see," said Sarah.

David piped in, "Zane, the guys at work have a lottery pool that they want me to join for ten dollars a week. It's only ten dollars. And if I do win, I would be able to put a good chunk into our savings fund. Should I join in with them?"

He was surprised to see Zane shaking his head vigorously.

"Saving your ten dollars a week will help you obtain your goal of being a millionaire every time. The chances of you winning a million are very, very, very slim. As a matter of fact, you have a higher chance of being struck by lightning. I personally call the lottery system a voluntary tax. You see, the proceeds from lotteries go to some good projects. The problem is that it's the poor and middle classes who primarily play the lottery who are funding projects. The wealthy do not play the lotteries; they earn their millions. By the way, did you know that most lottery winners are broke within a few years?"

"I have heard cases of that," replied David slowly.

"This is because the poor habits the winners had with only a little money generally carry over and amplify when they have a lot of money."

"Wow, I never thought of it that way," David said.

As the three were finishing up their poutine, Sarah explained that they had gotten their wills completed and had $500,000 life insurance policies for each of them. Zane smiled and said, "I love working with people who are teachable and put their learning into action. Keep up the good work!" He took one last bite, wiped his mouth with his napkin, and stacked his food carton onto Sarah's empty one. "I have an important appointment to go to now."

Sarah and David nodded their heads. "The girls are waiting for you?"

"That's right," said Zane as he got up from the picnic table and jumped in his Maserati. David stared as the Maserati jumped to life, and Zane waved as he peeled out onto the highway.

David turned to Sarah and said, "That car is way cool."

Sarah just smiled at him, put the trash in the can and headed toward Canadian Tire.

Saturday

A great night last night! David brought home steaks and wine as we paid off our first debt and celebrated. Paying of debt and feeling secure just puts me in the mood more often. I think David is liking the added bonus.

Saturday

Got lots of work done around the house today and ran into Zane coaching soccer. He really is a gifted coach. I am so glad we helped him change a tire that evening so long ago!

His Advice:
- We need wills and life insurance!
- Will:
  - get it done professionally by a lawyer for $500
  - get them to include future children/grandchildren
  - each of us needs:
    - a living will: state desires for medical

decisions, give signing
authority to spouse to
make medical decisions
- power of attorney to
spouse: spouse has
right to sign in property
matters
- <u>Life Insurance</u>:
- most people have too little
or no insurance, or buy
the wrong type!
- Don't go for insurance that
has a savings component,
cash value, or repayment
premiums if we won't use
it = expensive
- "Buy term insurance and
invest the rest"
- Don't buy mortgage
insurance unless we don't
qualify medically for term
insurance but don't have
to qualify medically for
mortgage insurance
- Problems with mortgage
or loan life insurance - 1.
more expensive than term
2. amount of insurance
coverage decreases as your
mortgage or loan is paid
down

- Insurance sales people oversell?? – No – most people are underinsured
- Guideline: each person should get 10x the highest income earner's gross salary
- <u>Term insurance:</u>
  - the longer the term, the higher the monthly premium
  - make sure it is guaranteed renewable at the end of the term
  - don't pay extra for the insurance to increase if it is accidental death
  - check to see if your company has term insurance. If so, make sure you can keep it when you leave. If not, take it as a bonus and get own insurance
- When we have larger assets, no debt, and no dependents, we don't need life insurance i.e. Million invested

NOTE: Call lawyer on Monday to book an appointment and look for insurance broker

Monday

More new things: David got a new job with Coke! He makes $3 more an hour. So far he seems to like it. Also, I am finding I don't go to the mall hardly ever anymore. The funny thing I discovered is environment is more powerful than will power... If I'm not in the stores, I don't need willpower.

Tuesday

David and I are doing so well! Was great to pass my second exam towards getting my real estate license. And we're ahead of schedule on our payment plan. I feel on top of the world.

Saturday

Boo. My car broke down today. I am so glad it is just an inconvenience and not a financial crisis anymore. Thanks Zane for our emergency cushion.

Saturday

David brought home flowers last night to celebrate paying off another debt. Life sure is more peaceful and light. We ran into Zane in Kemptville again.

    His advice:
- "You reap what you sow" - power of a positive attitude or a YES! attitude.
- Stay the course! Keep up with the payment schedule until debt is gone. Then, 1. increase savings with Coke to max they will match and 2. increase giving up to 10% point
- "A person convinced against his will is of the same opinion still"
- No lottery! Poor man's tax!!

Zane was sweet and treated us to poutine for dinner. We offered to pay, and he refused as usual. I think he is just as delighted to eat with us as we are to eat with him! He is so encouraging and full of wisdom.

David sure loves Zane's sportscar. I love watching his eyes light up whenever he sees the Maserati! I can't help dreaming of when we can afford luxuries like that. As life is getting more comfortable, I'm feeling more and more this maternal feeling, like I want a baby. Would probably make David choke if I brought the idea up. Will bide my time and maybe suggest it when our debts are paid off.

MY DECISIONS AND ACTION ITEMS.

Do I have adequate life insurance?

Are my wills and power of attorney done and up to date? Make an appointment with a lawyer if not.

What was my first debt I paid off or will pay off?

What will be my celebration?

Do I play the lottery and will I continue?

Do I understand critical illness and disability insurance and do I have or want any?

A coach can help me get back on track. Do I need any of the following coaches;

- Financial Coach,
- Life Coach,
- Fitness Coach,
- Spiritual Coach,
- Business Coach,
- Relationship Coach

A SETBACK IS A SETUP FOR A COMEBACK... FOURTH GEAR

Summer passed quickly and so did a few more of their debts. With the extra $100 and the laser focus effect, the first credit card, Sarah's car, and the second credit card were now paid off. It was amazing to Sarah that they now had $1961 a month to place on their last two debts. "At this rate David, we'll be done paying our taxes in a little over a month, and the guy at the taxation office will quit calling me and asking us to pay it off and…"

David cut her off, "It'll only take another three months and my car will be paid off, and we'll be consumer debt free."

"That's absolutely right!" said Sarah.

Several more weeks went by and it was time to put the bike away for another season. David finished hanging up the bike in the garage and headed in to see what Sarah was up to. As David walked into the living room, Sarah was sitting on the couch with a perplexed look on her face.

"What's up?"

"I think I just made a mistake," she said.

"What?" inquired David.

Sarah continued, "I got a phone call from someone who said we had been selected to win a free prize and that it would be at minimum a watch, but it could be a trip or a large screen TV. All we had to do was drive up to their resort next Saturday and listen to a 90 minute presentation."

"Is that all?" mused David. "I don't mind going to cottage country next week. It'll be good for us to get out. Besides, we have a celebration to have, so we can go out for a nice lunch and make an adventure of it."

"Okay," agreed Sarah gratefully, "I feel better now."

Saturday morning came, and it was cold but sunny and bright. David waited impatiently in the car until Sarah popped out of the house with two travel mugs of steaming hot coffee. "Oh, Sarah! Good thinking!" said David as he opened his lid and took a deep sniff.

"We save so much money a month when we just make our coffee, eh?" asked Sarah.

"We definitely do," replied David. "We just saved ourselves at least three dollars today alone!"

"Not to mention what we would have paid for these!" Sarah exclaimed as she shook two tupperware containers of crackers and cheese.

"You're so right. I would definitely get hungry and be stopping at the gas station for chips. Good thinking, honey."

"That's why you pay me the big bucks," grinned Sarah as she strapped herself in.

Sarah navigated and David drove. "I wish we had a GPS," said Sarah as she frowned at the paper in front of her. "It would be a lot easier."

"Yes it would," answered David. "And yet people have been getting around for years using this old fashioned piece of paper called a map. If we want to save for one later we can, but I don't think it's worth going into debt to buy one."

"Definitely not." She squinted and turned the map. "Okay, we need to go left on Zealand Road. It should be the next one."

David stretched in his seat and adjusted his hands on the wheel. He looked deep in thought for a moment. "You know, Sarah, it really wouldn't be worth going into debt for a GPS. Because, in Ontario with the HST set at 13%, it would take almost $300 of earnings to buy a $150 GPS."

"What? No, surely not."

"No really," said David. "It goes like this; if I earn $300 extra at work at the tax bracket that I am at now with all the overtime and my second job, I pay 42% combined tax to the federal government and provincial government." He paused again as he recalculated the math. "This means I would pay $126 on the $300, which would leave $174 after tax. Now the $150 GPS plus the 13% HST tax of $19.50 comes to $169.50, which is only $4.50 less then my after tax income. If you add on the gas to go buy the GPS, the $300 is gone."

Sarah shook her head, "That is wild!"

David was on a roll. "It's even worse when we go out for dinner, because we usually leave a 10% to 20% tip on the bill." David got a little funny smirk on his face, "Just imagine if we put the GPS on a credit card and were paying 18% interest on top of all that!"

Sarah shook her head again. "Unbelievable. I bet when most people go shopping they have no idea of what the true cost of things really is."

One hour later David and Sarah pulled into the parking lot of a beautiful resort. They got out and were welcomed into the reception area. The receptionist filled out a form with personal information on them. Things like: Did they travel at least one week a year? Were they over 25 years of age? Did they earn over $60,000 combined income? What were their jobs? etc. After this the couple were led into a large dining room where they met a friendly man with bushy eyebrows. His name was Ron. Ron explained that they would first have something to eat before he would take them on a tour of the facilities and then give them a short presentation. Lastly, they would draw for the prize.

"Seems simple enough," said Sarah.

During lunch, Ron continued to ask them about their family, where they had traveled in the past, and so on. He was a very nice man Sarah thought to herself. After lunch they went for their tour. The accommodations were deluxe, complete with a fireplace, kitchen, two bathrooms and two bedrooms. The grounds were beautifully landscaped, and the view, well let's just say it was a million dollar view. The lake was sparkling clean, and there was a small mountain with cleared sections for ski slopes. They noticed the chair lifts.

Back in the dining area, Ron explained that there was a championship golf course as well. He continued to explain that to own a chalet like this one would be very expensive, so a concept called time share/vacation club had been invented where families basically only paid for the portion that they were going to use each year.

"That makes sense," the couple murmured to each other.

After some more explaining, Ron said, "I have an offer for you."

David and Sarah looked at each other, "We thought you might."

Ron explained the pricing and maintenance fees and then explained that the great thing was that they could exchange their unit's week for other units around the world. It looked pretty intriguing, and David was excited about the concept but knew that they were not going to be buying today. Ron continued the presentation. "I can see you folks are a really nice couple, and I'd like to do you both a favour." He leaned across the table and offered them a deep discount to purchase.

David shook his head first as the amount of money was still too high, and they were determined not to go into debt. Ron explained that they could go to every other year and significantly break the price down.

Sarah reached down to collect her purse. "We'll need to think about it."

"Okay, no problem," Ron smiled. "I'd just like you to meet my manager."

Ron called over a middle aged smiling lady with bleached blonde hair and introduced her as Shirley. Shirley went back through the presentation and asked what was stopping them from making a decision.

David was quick to reply, "We don't have the cash."

"No problem! We have a payment plan."

This time Sarah responded, "We don't do credit, and we need to think about it."

Shirley nodded knowingly and continued, "I understand. What if we did this…We can take an additional 25% off."

"Wow, that is a really good deal," said David.

Sarah looked at David uncomfortably, "We still need to think about it."

Shirley smiled and started to stand. "Take your time, but know that once you leave the grounds, this offer will not be coming on the table again. It costs us a lot of money to get people here with the marketing and prizes, so we are only authorized to do this once. I'll give you some time to discuss it."

Sarah and David leaned in together to discuss back and forth at a present focus payment how long it would take to pay for the timeshare. After much debate Sarah said, "We should ask Zane."

"But we can't reach him," said David. "We only have today to get a deal this good."

Sarah looked around the room again, remembering the luxurious surroundings. She imagined having a reason to fly to Florida or Cancun every year. "You're right, let's do it," Sarah agreed reluctantly. It didn't feel right in her gut, but seemed reasonable in her head.

David and Sarah called Shirley over, and after she asked for their business again, the couple conceded that they could not give up such a good deal. David and Sarah signed the contracts, wrote a cheque for $400 for the down payment and arranged the financing plan. They drew a number for their prize and received a watch. Sarah selected a lady's model. They took the watch and headed for the car.

On the way home Sarah asked, "Did we just do a stupid thing? This watch sure is cheap. It feels like a $5.00 watch."

"I think we did okay. Let's talk with your parents after church this Sunday."

The couple were quiet the rest of the way home.

After a lunch of cold cuts and pea soup, David explained what had happened. Ruth was the first to speak, "Did you feel pressured?"

The couple nodded.

Ruth continued, "Did you doubt that you were doing the right thing? Would you do it over if you had a second chance?"

Sarah and David looked at each other for a moment and agreed they wouldn't.

"Ok, then, you made a mistake. Remember a setback is a setup for a comeback."

Sarah's head dropped. "But I feel so stupid," she moaned. David rubbed her shoulder. He looked equally unhappy.

"Don't feel bad," Mike soothed, spooning ice cream into small bowls. "We did the same thing several years ago and bought a timeshare too. Now we pay $400 a year in maintenance fees, whether we go on vacation or not. It kind of forces us to take holidays, which is okay for us, but it's much more expensive then just finding a last minute deal."

David sighed. "At the beginning I knew the price was just not worth it, but then when they kept lowering it, it seemed like we were getting a really good price. We didn't want to walk out and miss out on that deal."

Mike rubbed his hands together. "Let's take a look at the contract to see if there is an out or not. I suspect there might be, and it will likely come with a penalty."

As Michael read the contract, Sarah and Ruth made tea and put out some cookies. "I think I have found the 'out'," he said. "It says that within 48 hours of signing the documents, you can be released from the contract, yet your deposit will be kept as an administration fee."

"I think it's better to loose the $400 and consider it a good lesson learned." said Sarah.

"I think you're right," agreed David. "I'd rather loose $400 now than be tied into something that'll cost us thousands of dollars that we really cannot afford, and $400 a year whether we use it or not."

"I think that's wise," Michael replied. "I always say the best education I ever got was at the school of hard knocks. It seems that many times the painful lessons are the ones I learned the most from. You'll need to write a letter and fax it to the company first thing Monday morning before the 48 hours expire." He continued, "I'd also phone and request a receipt of them receiving the document faxed back to you. This way there can be no argument later."

The next few months whizzed by without incident except for the head gasket going in David's car. With other incidentals, it was a $2,000 unexpected expense that they had prepared for and therefore had the cash to cover the repair.

Spring was in the air in April, and the smell of wet leaves floated through the door as David came home one evening with a huge smile on his face. "I can't believe how our lives have changed," he said shaking his head with disbelief.

Sarah closed the oven she was cleaning and turned to face her husband. "What do you mean?" she asked.

Well," he continued, "today I ran some errands."

"Okay," Sarah prompted.

"Well, one was to the bank that holds my car loan, and I paid it off!" He picked up Sarah like she was a rag doll and spun her around so many times that they both collapsed into a dizzy heap on the couch.

As Sarah regained her equilibrium, it hit her. "David this means we are completely consumer debt free!"

David grinned from ear to ear, "That's right honey, we are debt free!"

"This is amazing," Sarah beamed. "And now that I'm done my third real estate course, all we are waiting on is the application for my license to be sent in by Keller Williams Solid Rock Realty."

"Oh?" asked David. "You've decided which brokerage to join then?"

"Yes," Sarah answered climbing onto his lap. "I checked out five of the main brokerages in town. Keller Williams Solid Rock Realty is where Yetta works. It had the best training, felt like a family atmosphere when I went there, and had a very competitive compensation plan. Plus on top of it all, they offered profit sharing."

"Sounds really good," David replied. "I'm so proud of you for passing your exam while still going to work part time."

"Thanks," said Sarah as she received a big kiss from David.

After David pulled himself away from Sarah, he patted her leg. "I have more good news, actually. I brought our taxes into the accountant last week and because of the $1,200 we gave to charity last year and the $2,400 we put into RRSP's, we didn't have to pay any extra income tax. As a matter of fact, we have about $300 coming back."

"Wonderful!" Sarah blurted out as she locked lips with her husband again.

"What do you want for dinner?" David asked.

Sarah smiled as she playfully bit David's shoulder. "I want you," she purred.

"Okay," he said as he picked her up and carried her up the stairs to their bedroom.

As they lay in each other's arms, Sarah sighed contentedly. "It feels so much easier to lie down and rest now that I know we have no more consumer debt and that we are in control of our finances." David hugged her more tightly and she continued. "I just have a new peace that I haven't experienced before. I can't quite explain the feeling."

"That's okay," David responded, "I think I understand. I know the feeling. I've had that same peace all day. I hope it never goes away."

"Me too," Sarah murmured.

The next morning David woke up to the smell of bacon cooking in the kitchen. He came down to find Sarah ready for the day and a wonderful breakfast. There was crispy bacon, whole grain toast, eggs perfectly basted sunny side up, and home fries from the left over potatoes from two nights earlier. "Wow," David exclaimed, "this is a wake up fit for a king."

"Yes it is," Sarah replied. "I thought you'd be hungry after missing dinner last night."

"I sure am, Sarah. I worked up some appetite." He gave her a kiss. David sat down, looked at the eggs, and said, "How did you learn to make perfect eggs like this?"

"My dad taught me how," replied Sarah. "I'll teach you next time we make eggs so that sometime you can make them for me." "Sounds good," said David.

While they ate, David looked pensive. "Hey Sarah, I've been thinking. Now that we are consumer debt free, we need to look at our budget again. You're going to need a car for Real Estate, and we now have about $2,500 each month that we haven't ear marked in the budget.

"You're right David," Sarah replied, taking a sip of her orange juice. "I was hoping we would see Zane sometime soon, and in the meantime I thought we should just keep it in the savings account. What so you think David?"

"I was hoping to buy a snowmobile sometime soon," he replied with a sheepish grin on his face. "But, I know that won't be the best use of that money right now, and I think what you suggested would be the wisest. This Saturday, I'll get the bike out of storage and we can go looking for Zane."

"That would be really nice," Sarah smiled with anticipation of getting back out on the bike. It had been a long winter.

Tuesday

Wow— the time share process sure was a learning experience. I am trying to NOT think about the number of shoes I could have bought with that penalty we had to pay — and focus instead on how much the experience will have saved us in the future. When I think of it that way, I'm so grateful we got out with only $400 in costs.

Hard to believe that our debt is gone except for our mortgage! The laser focus thing is amazing. I feel playful, energetic, and full of love. Can life get any better?

MY DECISIONS AND ACTION ITEMS.

What from previous chapters did I skip and need to go back and do?

Have I cheated the budget and need to ask for forgiveness?

What course could I take to better myself?

What is the next audio book I am going to listen to in the car?

What decisions have I made based on this chapter?

FIFTH GEAR

Saturday came and it was a glorious day. David had a plan that Sarah didn't know about. He got up early and prepared a picnic lunch of carrot sticks and cucumber slices with ranch dressing, a bag of potato chips, turkey sandwiches with lettuce, mayonnaise, and honey mustard, brownies and a bottle of Coke. David had the lunch all packed and ready to go and was started on making some oatmeal when Sarah came down for breakfast. There was a newness to her look, a glow in her complexion, a smile that could melt ice, and she had scrunched her hair with product. David admired her as she pulled the chair up to the island.

"What's for breakfast?" she inquired.

"What, no kiss and a hug?" David asked. It had become a ritual for them to have a ten second kiss and a thirty second hug every morning and every evening before bed.

Sarah leapt out of her chair and into David's arms for a long embrace and her ten second kiss. After, David gently pushed Sarah away. "What?! You don't like my kisses?" she pouted playfully.

David smirked. "It's that I like them too much; if we kiss more than ten seconds, you may not get breakfast, and it'll mess up my plans for this morning."

"What plans?" Sarah quizzed.

"I made your favourite for breakfast: oatmeal," David replied.

"Okay, but that's not a plan. What's the plan?" Sarah questioned.

"Oh, it's not important."

"Yes it is! What plans?!" Sarah loved surprises but did not like waiting for them.

David finally told her they were going on a bike ride.

"I figured that," Sarah answered with frustration in her voice.

"The rest is a surprise," David replied.

"Oh David, you are such a romantic," said Sarah half contentedly, half sarcastically.

"I know," David replied with a wink.

After a quick breakfast, David strapped the basket lunch onto the bike and off they went. As they started to head north, Sarah tapped David on the shoulder and asked again where they were going.

"It is a surprise," came back the response.

"Okay, then I'm going to tickle you all the way to where we are going!" Sarah announced.

"That's fine," teased David. "I can take that kind of torture."

For about an hour they generally rode in a northern direction with a few turns thrown in to throw Sarah off the scent of where they were going. "Are we going to my parents house?" she questioned.

"No."

After about an hour of peddling they rolled into Osgoode Village.

"Are we staying in Osgoode?"

David nodded. They saw a lot of commotion happening around the community centre. Sarah realized that it was an antique and muscle car show. "That is what you made me wait all morning for? Cars?!" she exclaimed. She gave David a sharp punch in the shoulder.

His torso jerked and roughly wobbled the bike so that they almost tumbled off. As David was righting the front wheels, they hit a curb and both tumbled off. They got up disheveled and laughing until it hurt.

After Sarah calmed down, David said, "Don't worry, Sarah, there is more to the surprise."

"What?" Sarah inquired

"Can you keep a secret?"

"I sure can!"

"So can I!" replied David and dodged another playful punch to the shoulder. "Missed me!" he teased as Sarah started to chase him.

David let Sarah eventually catch him and they wrestled for a little while until David locked her in his arms. He whispered in her ear, "I love it when you are so light and playful."

Sarah turned in his arms to face him, pretended to want to kiss him and playfully bit his bottom lip until David had no choice by to cry 'uncle.' After letting his slightly red lip loose, Sarah said, "I just feel so free and alive since all our debts are gone! Now, all we have left is the mortgage on our little house that you have been working so hard to make into a home."

"I know what you mean," David said with a little lisp as his bottom lip was a little numb and swollen. "I've been feeling a lighter step in my walk. It feels like a large part of the load to provide for our family has been lifted from my shoulders."

Sarah gave him one last kiss before breaking free from his embrace and heading for the cars. Sarah had paused at a stunning 1962 Corvette. It was a convertible in powder blue with a fresh dark blue interior, including leather buckets. David caught up to her and was admiring the vette himself.

"My dad always wanted one of these," she said walking around the car. "He almost bought one when he was 16 years old, but his dad taught him that you shouldn't buy a car unless you can pay cash. Someday I'm sure he'll get one."

Her voice drifted off as she headed towards a 1968 Camaro RS SS that was also a convertible. It was done up in candy apple red with the black striping typical of the RS SS model. David had his eye on a 1968

Firebird 400. As she wandered over, David wrapped his arm loosely over her shoulders and said, "Just look at this black beauty; it's over 40 years old and looks like the day it came out of the show room except for a few modern additions like disc brakes and these chrome wheels. Somebody really knows how to care for a car."

"Thank you," replied the owner.

David whipped around at the sound of the familiar voice and saw Zane walking towards them. "What?" he exclaimed. "Is this your car?"

"It sure is," said Zane.

Sarah smirked at David's dropped jaw and gave him a little nudge. "Is this the way you greet a friend?" She greeted Zane with a hug.

David sheepishly said hello and gave him one of those manly hugs where you tap each other on the back a couple of times. David pulled back and mused at how close the three of them were becoming through their chance encounters.

Zane grinned happily. "You want to see the engine?"

"Sure would," was the reply from Sarah before David could get a word out.

Zane popped the hood, and David was almost blinded by the sun reflecting off the chrome in the engine compartment.

"Is this the original engine?" asked David.

Zane nodded. "I had a complete frame off restoration done last year, and while it was apart I had the engine rebuilt, the block was painted, and I had every part that could be chrome plated done at a great factory in Montreal."

Since the hood was opened, the 68 bird began attracting quite a crowd. As they were rounding out the tour by looking at the meticulously maintained trunk, Zane said, "I'm getting a little hungry. Would you like to go for a drive and pick up some food?"

David jumped at the opportunity. "I have a picnic lunch packed on the bike, and there's plenty for three. Why don't I grab it, and we can head down to Taylor Park for lunch and watch the boats go by?"

"Great idea." Zane closed the trunk and hood, opened the door for Sarah to get in, and then fired up the engine while they waited for David.

David climbed in with the basket on his lap, and they slowly made their way through the crowd to the road. A few people yelled, "Light her up!" as Zane pulled onto the road.

Zane shook his head good naturedly. As he stepped on the gas, there was a small chirp from the rear tires, and then another chirp as he changed into second gear. Zane put on the breaks as he noticed he was already exceeding the speed limit.

"Have you ever opened her up?" David inquired.

"Oh yes," came a gleeful reply. "After I had the engine rebuilt, I took her up to a track in Calabogie where you can really test out a car and not be on public roads breaking any laws. It was a ton of fun. There were all kinds of people up there test racing their sport cars."

"Sounds like a lot of fun," David said, "and cheaper in the long run than getting tickets and demerit points."

"Not to mention not endangering the lives of other people," murmured Sarah teasingly.

"It's true," said David as memories of his many traffic tickets surfaced in his mind.

David pointed across River Road, "There it is, Zane. Just pull in there and park to the right."

The three climbed out of the car that now had a few specs of dust on it. David apologized for the dirt.

"Oh that's no problem," Zane said, "I detail her every time I bring her home from a drive."

David spotted an empty picnic table by the water's edge and headed that way. By the time Sarah and Zane got to the table, David had already begun to spread out the feast he had prepared.

Zane asked if it would be alright to say grace. He gave thanks for the food, the many blessings God had bestowed on them, and for His magnificent creation. They opened their eyes and saw a mallard duck swimming by with six little ducklings following her in a neat line. As the three enjoyed their lunch and the view of the river, Sarah excitedly recapped what they had accomplished in such a short time.

"I knew you would," said Zane. "This means you are ready to shift into fifth gear of the process."

"What's that?" said David.

"Well, this one is fairly easy because you now have a significant amount of positive cash flow per month."

"We sure do," piped up Sarah. "We have about $2500 per month that we have available."

Zane smiled, "That's a lot of loose cash each month. So, you remember step one."

"We sure do. Build a $2000 emergency fund."

"That's right," Zane smiled again. "I told you that was your cushion, and now it's time to have a four to six months of expenses emergency fund saved up. I call it your whoopee cushion."

David chuckled at the image.

Sarah wanted clarification. "So, we put the $2500 towards building up 4 to 6 months of expenses in reserve?"

"Well, almost," replied Zane. "It's like this. You guys have done a fantastic job of permanently eliminating consumer debt from your lives; now that you have some breathing room, it's time to bump up your budget in the three areas that had percentages beside them."

"You mean wealth building, savings, and giving," David said.

"Good for you," Zane replied. "Yes, it's time to make your giving 10% of your gross income, wealth building 10% of your gross income, and savings to be 5% of your net."

"Why are the first two on your gross?" Sarah asked.

"Well, God said in the Bible to give of the first fruits, which is in my opinion before the government gets their taxes. By the way, does the government tax you on your gross or your net?"

"On the gross, of course," David said.

"Right, so why not give on the gross? Besides the government gives you a tax break on your charitable giving, so it's tax free money you are giving away. Also, the wealth building is on the gross because as long as you are in the highest tax bracket, I'm going to recommend that you put your wealth building money in an RRSP account for a while anyways until it is a significant amount of money."

"Why only if we are in the highest tax bracket?" Sarah asked.

"It's a little complicated," said Zane. "I'll try to make it simple. The highest tax bracket right now is about 42% in Ontario when you include federal and provincial tax."

"My income tax isn't 42%," David said.

"That's right," Zane said. "We have a graduated taxation system in Canada where your first several thousands are tax free. Then, as you earn more money, you'll pay a higher percentage on the money over certain thresholds, so although you don't pay 42% on all the money you make, the last dollars you make are taxed in the highest bracket.

"Charity, except for the first $200, is tax deductible at your highest tax bracket, and your RRSP's are tax deductible at your highest taxable rate. In other words, they come off the top and could effectively bring you down into a lower tax bracket."

"I think we're following," Sarah said, "but I still don't understand why we should put our money into an RRSP only if we are in a high tax bracket?"

"Well, it's because an RRSP is not tax free; it's tax deferred," replied Zane.

Now both Sarah and David looked puzzled.

"It is like this," Zane continued. "When you put money in an RRSP, it is temporarily tax free, and an interesting thing is that all the growth or income on the money is temporarily tax free. When you reach age 70, you have to start removing a percentage of your RRSP or you decide to retire and want to draw on your RRSP. At that time, whatever you draw out each year is taxable at the highest tax bracket that you are then in. Most people say that they will be in a lower tax bracket because they are retired. If you follow my wealth building formula, you will have so much cash flow that you will be in the highest tax bracket when you retire."

"I think I get it," David said slowly.

"Let me put it this way. Let's say at retirement your net worth is $4,000,000."

"Are you kidding?" asked Sarah with eyes as wide as saucers.

"No, I'm not," smiled Zane. "You're well on your away to being multimillionaires if you stay with the program."

"Okay!" said David as he leaned forward towards Zane, "I don't care if this river floods and washes us and these ducks away! I'm listening."

Zane chuckled. "Remember I said your wealth building account would never be spent by you?"

"Yes," answered David.

"This is why. Many people retire with an amount of money that they hope will last them until they die. The problem with that is many people out live their money, or one partner requires long term care. This is very expensive, and they use up the retirement fund, only to leave the other spouse with no money left and no idea of how long they are going to live beyond their spouse. In other words, to borrow from the children's story about the goose that laid the golden eggs, your retirement fund should be the goose and you should live on the eggs. Or, living on the income, not on the principal. If you use the principal, you are slowly killing the goose.

"Let's say of the $4,000,000, two million is in assets that don't make an income like your house, cars, vacation property, furniture, jewelry etc.

They're still worth two million if you sold them, yet they don't produce income, and as a matter of fact, most of them cost you money each month in insurance, maintenance etc. Now, the other two million is in income and growth investments that are returning 12% per year. That would bring $240,000 a year or $20,000 per month. Do you think you could live on that a month with no debt, no car payments, and no mortgage payment?"

"You bet we could!" said Sarah. "And we could do even more charity work with the money that we don't need to live."

David spoke up. "Yeah, but how in the world are we going to earn 12% per year?"

"There are many ways the wealthy earn that and much more, but that's for another lesson when you are financially ready for overdrive. We haven't even gotten into sixth gear yet."

"Zane, you make learning about money so much fun," said Sarah. "I used to zone out when my parents used to talk to me about money. I never thought it could be so interesting."

"Thanks," replied Zane. "Speaking about interesting, did you know that about 90% of the world's population has 10% of the world's wealth, and in contrast, 10% of the population has 90% of the wealth?"

"Seriously?" asked David. "Why is it like that?"

"Well," Zane replied after a while, "I guess it's partly because only a small percentage are willing to learn how to build wealth and have the discipline to live it out day by day. They work hard to make sure that their money works for them and that it's not them working for money."

Looking out over the river Zane smiled again. "We're on this side of the river. Let's pretend our side represents the 90% that have 10% of the wealth. People on this side of the river make money by being employed or self employed. On the other side of the river are the 10% with 90% of the wealth. They typically own a business and income generating assets."

"Is not being self employed owning a business?" Sarah thought out loud as she was now self employed as a REALTOR®.

"No," replied Zane. "Many self employed people think they own a business. A business makes money and continues to operate smoothly whether or not the owner shows up for work or not. In contrast, a self employed person's income stops if they are not working."

"I see," said Sarah.

"Now, if most of the wealth is on the other side of the river, why do you think so few cross the river?" queried Zane.

After a long pause David spoke up. "I guess because they're afraid to swim across or don't have a boat."

"You're absolutely right. They think the water is too deep and too far to swim. There may be crocodiles in the water, and they aren't willing to build a boat," Zane said excitedly.

"Now you've really lost me," Sarah said.

Zane calmed down and then said, "What's in the water is fear, doubt, bad habits, consumer debt, pessimism, risk. That's what prevents many from trying to cross, and ignorance or poor work habits drown others who try to cross. So to make it across safely, you need a boat, and in your boat, you'll need knowledge, wisdom, good discipline, mentors, a support team, and cash flow.

"Let me explain. Knowledge is obtained by learning. One of the best ways to learn a subject is to read twelve books on that subject. So, if you want to learn money management and wealth building strategies, read twelve books on the subject. Say one a month. Did you know it only takes about twenty to thirty minutes a day to read a book a month? Many people spend 3-4 hours a day watching TV and movies. Wisdom is how you use your attained knowledge and experiences to make great decisions. Good discipline will keep you healthy and also prevent you from going into debt for consumer wants, which is the easiest way to put a big hole in your boat. Mentors are people who have crossed the river before and can show you the way. A support team is something everyone needs. When it comes to wealth building, your support team will need the following great professionals in it; a lawyer, accountant, estate planner, Realtor, investment advisor, mortgage broker and insurance agent. Don't go cheap on your support team; seek out and hire a great support team because their expertise is worth every penny. Think of it like climbing Mount Everest; the higher the goal, the need for a great team increases.

Finally, cash flow is the fuel for the engine. You need to work at increasing your income and putting more into your investments. The average person thinks of their paycheck as a supply house. It's used to meet their daily needs, wants, and debt repayment. I like to think of my pay cheque as a sack of seeds. First of all, the larger I can make the sack of seeds each week, the better. You can seek a raise at work."

"That's hard to do, is it not?" interrupted Sarah.

"Not as hard as you'd think," replied Zane. "The secret is to ask first what your boss sees as your primary job description. Many are working hard but not at what the company would like to achieve. Then ask if time permitted what would be ideal for the company to achieve through your efforts. Now, focus on those things for the next three months and then ask for a raise. Secondly, ask your boss what course he or she would recommend to benefit your career path and the company's. Let your bosses know that you want to advance and are willing to work hard, smart, and on your off time to achieve your goal."

"I see," said David.

"Now," Zane continued, "you are working at enlarging your sack of seeds. You will only be using some of your seed money to live on, none for debt repayment, and as much as possible will be seed that goes into your wealth building account. And of course some will go into your savings accounts to purchase those larger items in the future that you will need and want, and to increase your emergency fund, or as I call it, your whoopee cushion."

"How do we know what amounts for each?" Sarah asked.

Zane smiled and replied, "I like to use percentages because as long as you begin early enough to take advantage of the compounding effect, it doesn't matter too much how much you earn. If you're content with your lifestyle under the budget, you'll also be content with your income at retirement. What I mean is that if you are satisfied with your current cash flow, then you can save in your permanent wealth account twelve times your yearly expenses. Then at 10 to 12% rate of return, you'll earn enough each year to cover your life style and cover the rate of inflation if it stays around 2-3%. If inflation increases at a faster rate, it's important to understand that your fixed assets, like your home, vacation property, art, etc., will also be increasing in value at somewhere around the rate of inflation."

Sarah shook her head. "Zane, it just seems so far out of reach."

"I understand," said Zane. "You'll most likely not have the discipline to do it unless you have a big enough 'why'."

"What do you mean by 'why'," David asked.

"Well your 'why' is your reason for doing it," replied Zane. "For some, fear is a motivator, and for others, it is that status quo is not enough; they have a passion for the future. Remember your reason for getting out of debt."

"Do I ever," said David. "It was because the pain of being in debt and the stress and uncertainty was almost too much to bear, and it was affecting our marriage."

"Right," said Zane. "Is that pain gone?"

"Amazingly, it is!" said Sarah.

"So the pain is gone, and now there's nothing to propel you forward or to stop you from slipping backwards, so we need to create a way of creating a vision and passion for the future that will pull you forward even if and when you run into obstacles. I know two ways to create this in your life. The first is what I call the ultimate scenario letter. This is a letter to someone, maybe your future kids or to each other. Write out your letter like everything went perfectly for the next thirty years. Tell them what you do, where you live, what vacations you take, what you drive, what charities you support, and what your net worth is. Dream big and make sure you write your letter in past tense, as though you have already accomplished it. When you get it done, you should come back together and compare letters. They may be quite different. You'll need to then have a nice dinner and discuss each other's letters with the goal of writing a new letter that encompasses all of your dreams together. You need to be on the same page or you won't work together to accomplish the goal.

"The second method is one I used when I was first learning about these things. I took my journal and spent a couple of hours alone writing all the things I would like to accomplish before I die. Some people call it their 'Bucket List'. In other words, it's what I want to accomplish before I 'kick the bucket'."

David snorted.

"I set a goal of writing out 100 things I want to do before I die. It was a great exercise, and I often go back to that journal, which has long been filled with lessons I learned along the way, and check up on my list. It seems that each time I read it, I'm able to highlight a few more things that I have accomplished and add a few new ones to the list. This list for me is a fluid document. There are some items that I may never be able to accomplish, like wanting to go to Holland with my Dad. He passed away before I had a chance to do that one, and there may be some items on the list that have just lost their importance, and others that make the list as you grow and your priorities change."

"This sounds like fun," said Sarah.

"Yeah, and a lot of work," David chimed in.

"It's really worth it," Zane said, "and it's the next step for you to do before I can help you much more."

"Okay, okay," David said. "Whatever it takes, I'll do it."

"That's great," said Zane. "Okay, there's one more little lesson I'd like to teach you, and then I need to be off for a drive to the city. I have another important date."

"Another date with eighteen young ladies?" Sarah winked at Zane. She paused from her copious note taking.

"You're quite right. They're the young women in my life right now. I get such a kick out of coaching soccer. This is a great opening into the next lesson too. The next lesson is the 4 S's. Do you remember living from paycheque to paycheque?"

"Do we ever," Sarah said.

"Well the first S in the 4 S's is Survival. That's what you were in when we met. You have now moved into Stability, which is the second S. Stability is no consumer debt and one month's expenses saved as an emergency fund. The third S is Success, which is 3-6 months in an emergency fund and all your percentages going to giving, permanent wealth, and your savings account. The rest is what you are living on without using credit for anything, except investing or business. The final S is Significance. At this point, you have no debt and you have 12 years of expenses in your permanent wealth account."

"You mean we're going to have 12 years of expenses saved up in a bank account?" David asked with disbelief.

"No, it won't be in a bank account because that won't even keep up to inflation. Typically, I call it an account, as an accounting term not a physical account," Zane explained. "It will be in many different investments."

"I can't wait to learn how to invest and build wealth," David said eagerly.

"I know," Zane smiled. "And yet you will have to wait as I have to get going!"

The three gathered up the picnic basket and blanket and jumped back into the 400. David grinned from ear to ear as the car jumped to life with a beautiful sounding rumble when Zane turned the key. In just a minute they were back at the bike, and Zane's car was a distant memory as all David could see was the dust it kicked up as Zane zoomed away to his soccer game.

David and Sarah mounted the bike for their long trip home. Both were quiet as the lessons Zane had imparted to them rolled around in their heads. When they arrived home, they went to bed exhausted although it was only 7:30p.m..

"What an incredible day," David murmured to Sarah.

"Definitely was," she replied sleepily as she drifted off to sleep.

David lay there wide awake listening to his wife gently snore. He thought it sounded more like a contented cat's purr than a snore. David could not get the day and the tasks ahead out of his mind, so after about an half hour, he slipped his then asleep arm out from under Sarah's head and slowly rolled out of bed not to disturb her. David rummaged around in the kitchen until he found a three ring note book.

"This'll have to do until I can buy a journal," he thought as he sat down to write his ultimate scenario letter and his 100 things list. The hours flew by as he wrote, and wrote, and imagined, and dreamed. At around 3:30 a.m., David glanced at his watch with a yawn. "I've done some good work," he thought to himself as he put his journal away and quietly made his way up to bed. He fell asleep almost instantly.

Sarah woke up early Sunday morning around 4:30 a.m. and rolled out of bed. She didn't want to wake up David as he looked so deep in sleep. She thought to herself, "This will give me a chance to write what Zane had told us to do, and I can be ahead of David." Sarah was becoming quite competitive when it came to learning and getting thinking work done as she loved being organized. She pulled out her journal and began her list.

A few hours later she had it mostly finished. The idea that she might accomplish even half of the items astonished her. "This should make it easier to write the ultimate scenario letter now that I have this done," she thought. Sarah turned the page and started to write.

The next time she looked at the kitchen clock, it was 9:00 a.m.. "Oh!" she exclaimed, we have to get to church in half an hour."

She ran up stairs to wake up David. After several pushes and a few kisses, David stirred. "Get up," she bullied. "We have to leave for church in twenty five minutes."

David gave her a kiss and jumped into the shower. He loved going to church and connecting with family and friends. As he showered, he thought of the list he had prepared and how he was ahead of Sarah for once in his life.

On the way to church, Sarah couldn't keep it in anymore. She decided to take a very nonchalant approach and mention it very casually. "I finished the homework Zane gave us yesterday!" she blurted. So much for that idea.

"No way," said David. "You fell asleep as soon as we went to bed."

"I know," said Sarah, "but I got up at 4:30 to do it!" She tried to hide the smug smirk creeping into her features.

"I still beat you!" David said with a gleam in his eye. "I stayed up until 3:30 and finished mine. So technically, I finished before you."

"What?" she asked incredulously. "So, you were actually done before me?"

"That's right, Sarah dear! For once I beat you at something financial!"

"That's okay. I'm sure mine is better than yours anyway," she said as she gave David a very flirty look.

"Careful," he said, "I'm driving here."

Although Sarah and David were tired, the lively music and excellent message allowed them to stay awake during the church service. They were hoping that Sarah's parents would invite them back for lunch so that they could discuss their newfound method of planning for a fantastic life. Sure enough, Michael and Ruth invited the couple over for a hot lunch.

Right after praying for the food, Michael would normally start eating. Meal time was for eating; the talking did not come until the coffee had been passed around. Today was different; Mike immediately said to Sarah and David, "You guys look different. More relaxed, happy. Joyful even."

Sarah started first as David had a mouthful of pot roast. "We feel like we have a new fresh start on life," she explained. "We're now debt free, except for our mortgage, we have a couple months' expenses saved up in the bank, and we recently learned a new process to map out the things we would like to accomplish before we die. David and I spent half the night last night working through the process. Tonight we get to compare our goals to see what we plan to accomplish together."

"Wow," Ruth spoke up. "It sounds like you guys have accomplished in a couple of years what it took your father and I thirty years to accomplish."

"Really?" Sarah questioned. "You have a list of things you want to accomplish before you die?"

"We sure do," Ruth said. "Michael and I had a business coach fifteen years ago, and he taught us to write out the 100 things we want to do before we 'kick the bucket'.

"That's funny," David said. "That's exactly what Zane taught us to do."

Michael piped up, "Great minds think alike."

Sarah looked a little hurt. "Why have you never shared your list with me?"

"I guess we thought they were personal," said Michael as he got up from the table and excused himself. He was back in a moment carrying a black journal. He turned to the first couple of pages and showed it to Sarah and David. "I'm sorry that I haven't shown this to you before."

Sarah scanned the pages and noticed that the items were numbered between 1 and 135. About one third had colour highlighter on them and a couple had lines through them. "I guess the highlighted ones are the things you have accomplished, and the ones with the lines through them are those you don't want to do anymore?"

"Exactly," answered Mike. "You know the neat thing about this list? Every six months or so I pull it out, and there's usually one or two things I can highlight and a couple of things I can add. It seems that just reading the list every six months or so reinforces my subconscious to make decisions that help bring into my life the things on the list. I've accomplished so much over the last fifteen years that if I hadn't written the list, I highly doubt I would have done even 10% of the items I managed to do. You know what they say: Failing to plan is planning to fail."

After lunch Sarah and Ruth chatted about Sarah's list while David and Michael washed the cars and discussed David's list. After the cars were spotless, David pulled Sarah into a hug and mentioned it was probably time to go. "We still have to compare lists, and I'm already feeling tired."

Ruth couldn't resist. "You know, David, I've been reading a book on sleep patterns. It says that we sleep in 1½ hour cycles, and it's best if we wake up naturally at the end of a cycle. Some people need more or less but almost everyone does well on 7 ½ hours. It also says going to bed and waking up at the same time seven days a week is better as it helps your body become disciplined."

"Interesting," said David looking over to Sarah. "We should try that out for a few weeks and see how we do."

"I'm up for it," agreed Sarah. "This could be one of our new habits or disciplines that Zane has been talking about."

"Boy, that Zane sounds like quite the guy. I'd love to meet him sometime," said Michael.

There was an awkward pause. "Well that may be difficult," Sarah spoke first and broke the silence. "We don't know how to reach him; he just seems to show up when we're ready for the next step in our process of building wealth."

"That is kind of mysterious, isn't it?" mused Ruth.

"It is," said David, "and yet it's such a blessing to spend time with him that we haven't said anything. Zane is so wealthy and fairly busy and yet when ever we meet, he makes time for us. I think it's just who he is and not because I changed a tire for him a couple of years ago."

"You know, now that I think about it, Zane is very handy. I'm sure he could have changed his own tire very easily. It may have just been fate that we ran into him when we did."

"Or divine intervention," pondered Sarah.

Once home, David and Sarah spared no time comparing notes on their lists. About fifty percent of the items were on both lists. Sarah added some of David's to hers and David added some of Sarah's on his. When they were done, they had about 80 items on their lists with about 60 items being the same.

"This feels so neat," Sarah exclaimed. "I feel so connected to you, David. It's like our lives and goals are on the same page, and yet you and I have some things that each of us want to do individually that the other doesn't. This is going to be a fun journey."

"It definitely is," David replied. "I can't believe I might be able to buy a Maserati someday. I mean, I know anything is possible, but putting it on paper like that makes it seem...real. Like it is going to happen or something."

"I know what you mean. I never dreamed I could actually accomplish even a quarter of these things. But, if we focus on it, and take steps towards it, these things are within our reach."

"At least they are now that we are financially free," added David. "I look forward to adding new items. This is such a cool tool. Who knew your parents have been doing it for 15 years."

"Yeah, I know," said Sarah. "They must be doing a few things right. They're very well off and are always into learning."

"Ahh well I know one thing," yawned David as he stretched. "I definitely don't need dinner after that pot roast."

"Me neither," agreed Sarah. "I always overeat when Dad makes his famous gravy."

As they were laying there ready to sleep, David reminded her that the next day would be the first of the month.

"So what," she whispered dreamily.

"I get to figure out our net worth statement at the first of every month."

Sarah began to snore lightly. David laid his head back on his pillow. He realized that the wealth building part was up to him. Sarah didn't have a financial care in the world as long as she felt their future was secure and David was looking after the numbers.

Saturday

Debt is GONE!!! Was so excited to tell Zane about it today! David took me out as a surprise to a muscle car show and we ran into him. He drove us around in his Firebird, and we ate lunch in the park.

His Advice:
- Time to top up giving and wealth building to 10% of our gross each and savings to 5% of our net income

90% people	10% people
10% of the wealth	90% of the wealth
EMPLOYEES	BUSINESSES
SELF EMPLOYED	PASSIVE INCOME
" I work for my income "	" People and $$ work for me!"

- *** Need to build a BOAT to cross the river!!!
- Build it with KNOWLEDGE and WISDOM

- Fill it with CASH FLOW, GOOD DISCIPLINE, MENTORS and a team of EXPERTS to get us across the river to where the wealth is really built.
- Mentors = people who have crossed the river before you and can show you the way
- Expert support team = lawyer, accountant, estate planner, Realtor, investment advisor, mortgage broker, insurance agent, etc.
- Don't go cheap on the support team build a "Dream Team"!
- **Think of my pay cheque not as a supply house but as a SACK OF SEEDS!
- RRSP - good for people in highest tax bracket. If in lower tax bracket, use something else
- Buy a couple of the books Zane recommended. OOOh! LIBRARY! **

<u>Sunday</u>

My Ultimate Scenario Letter

My marriage is great after 25 years.
We live debt free, love the Lord,
and have 3 children that are also
following Christ. This has been the
best 25 years of my life. We live
in Manotick, have a lake house for
the summer, and a beach front for
winter. Life is beyond good!
David and I have broken the cycle
of debt. My children pay cash for
everything they want or do without.
Earned money is now not for survival,
stability or success. These are
taken care of! Money earned is
now because we want to work, not
because we have to, and wealth is
for the good it can do for others as
well.
We loan out our vacation properties
to pastors and missionaries. David
and I speak and teach regularly
on financial peace and marriage
relationships.

My Bucket List

1. Have children 2-6
2. Own a house in Manotick
3. Own a lake house

4. Give $10,000 away in one cheque
5. Support a village in Africa - self-sustaining methods
6. Own an Escalade SUV
7. Put children through college or university debt free!
8. Write a wealth building book for children
9. See where Jesus walked - Jerusalem, Galilee, etc.
10. Visit Hawaii
11. Buy an RV and travel North America
12. Fly in a helicopter over the Grand Canyon
13. Visit Australia and see a kangaroo
14. Visit the village in Africa
15. Go glacier trekking
16. Cruise Alaska
17. Cruise all the Caribbean Islands
18. Cruise the Mediterranean
19. Visit extended relatives in Denmark
20. Take a honeymoon to Jamaica
21. Build $4,000,000 net worth
22. Tithe 10% to church for the rest of my life
23. Buy a convertible
24. Own a boat
25. Go skiing in British Columbia

26. Go parasailing
27. Own a great real estate company
28. Sell 50 homes in one year!
29. Win annual Keller Williams Luxury Home Realtor award!
30. Learn to fly a plane, or at least take a lesson
31. Buy a speed boat
32. Read a book a month
33. Get my broker's license for real estate
34. Buy an investment home on the ocean somewhere warm
35. Have 10 investment properties
36. Stay below 120 lbs unless pregnant
37. Visit Rome and see the coliseum
38. Go rock climbing
39. Repel off a mountain
40. See the pyramids
41. Coach soccer
42. Teach swimming
43. Learn about being a great wife and mother
44. Do a public speaking engagement on marriage/relationships
45. Own a three carat diamond ring
46. Give $100 thousand away in one year
47. Learn to ballroom dance well

48. Learn Danish as a second language
49. Create at least 5 great lifelong friendships
50. Learn more about nutrition
51. Become a certified trainer for Keller Williams
52. Become a coach for Keller Williams
53. Spoil my grandchildren
54. Leave legacy fund for future generation
55. Walk the Great Wall of China
56. See Mayan ruins
57. Meet John Maxwell
58. Drive a race car in Calabogie
59. Pick bananas
60. Eat a fresh pineapple off the bush
61. Take a week long canoeing/ portage trip
62. Get an interior decorator to redo our house!
63. Go to Kingdom Bound at Darien Lake
64. Learn to play base guitar
65. Buy a Maserati
66. Buy a 62 Corvette for my dad
67. Travel with Dad to his hometown
68. Pick a coconut off a tree
69. Travel across Canada - coast to coast

70. See the Northern Lights
71. Go salmon fishing on the west coast
72. Grow orchids
73. Have a games room with a pool table, air hockey, darts, etc. for the kids
74. Build a fabulous home theatre room
75. Fly to the moon
76. Learn to paint
77. Flip a home as an investment project
78. Take my kids to Walt Disney World
79. Set up a scholarship for Bible college at church
80. Develop land into a subdivision

Write out my 100 things I want to do before I die.

Write out my ultimate scenario letter.

Share these two things with the person I am closest to.

What other actions do I want to take after reading this chapter?

What learning, relationship or changes do I need to make to my boat to cross the river?

PUTTING THE PEDAL TO THE METAL

After work on Monday, Sarah could not wait to share her news with David. When they both arrived home around the same time, David was grinning ear to ear.

"What's up?" Sarah quizzed.

"Well, I'm getting a raise at work of fifty cents an hour, which will mean we can save even quicker for that new to us vehicle you need."

"That's great news!" Sarah exclaimed.

"That's not all," David said. "You know how when we first did out net worth statement, it was a negative number?"

"How could I not remember that," Sarah replied with a sour look on her face.

David beamed now and blurted out, "Well, we just broke the $100,000 asset mark!"

"No way," stated Sarah. "How can that be?"

"Well," David answered, "We no longer pay interest, so that has cleared up about $1,000 a month, our cars are free and clear, the stock market had improved so my RRSP through work has gone up a lot, and our house has increased in value over the last couple of years by 12% per year, plus all the work we have done to it."

"This is wonderful!" Sarah exclaimed. "I never thought we could make so much progress in such a short amount of time! What Zane said about having a net worth of four million at retirement sure seems a little more in reach doesn't it?

"Sure does," David replied. "The only thing I don't know is how we are going to get and keep great returns like Zane talks about."

"Speaking of Zane," Sarah cut David off, "he called me at work and said we should go to the town dock in Iroquois for 7:00 p.m. Friday and to bring an overnight bag and bathing suits."

"This guy is unbelievable. I have no idea what he has up his sleeve." David cleared his throat as a lump had appeared in it. "You know, ever since I was a little kid, I always wanted to sleep on a boat."

"I remember it from your bucket list," said Sarah patting him on the back.

"Do you think that's what he has planned for us?"

"I'm not sure what it is, but I will tell you this: I'm going to bring my journal," Sarah answered. "I know when ever we see Zane he has wisdom to pass along."

"Me too," David said. "Me too."

Friday couldn't come fast enough for Sarah and David. That evening, both Sarah and David hurried home, had a quick dinner, and grabbed their bag, which Sarah had packed four days earlier. They jumped on the bike to make the hour long trek to the public dock. Sarah had never travelled that fast on the bike before. David must have been peddling hard as Sarah could see the back of David's shirt was soaked with sweat as they pulled into the park and headed towards the dock just a few minutes before seven.

David gasped as he saw a large cruiser docked at the dock. It was the only boat in sight. As they approached the dock, David and Sarah recognized Zane standing on the dock.

"Welcome," Zane hailed as the couple approached him.

"Hi," Sarah said.

"Is this yours?" asked David as Sarah gave him a mock punch in the shoulder and said "It is customary to say hello before one starts asking questions."

Zane laughed as David greeted him. He welcomed them on board and offered them a drink.

"I sure could use a Coke." said David. "It was quite the peddle from Brinston."

"Water would be great for me, Zane."

"Coming right up," announced Zane as he disappeared into the cabin area.

Moments later he appeared with the drinks as the engines on the boat came to life. Zane passed them the glasses, jumped off the boat to untie her, and then hopped back on and sat down on a bench next to David.

"Who's driving the boat?" David inquired.

"Oh the captain is driving. I don't feel comfortable driving such a large boat, and after all if I was driving I wouldn't have time to visit with you."

"That's nice," Sarah replied.

As the boat pulled away from the dock, David asked Sarah if it was okay to ask questions now as his shoulder was a little sore and he didn't want to invoke another left hook to his arm.

"Yes it is," she said with a flirty smile to David. David just loved that smile.

"How big is she?" David asked Zane.

"She is 38 feet," Zane replied.

"Do you own her?"

"I own a part of her."

Sarah was puzzled. She assumed the bank was the other owner, as with most of the big things her friends owned. She perked up. "I thought you didn't buy on credit?"

"I don't," said Zane.

"Then who owns it with you?" she asked.

"It's like this," Zane offered. "I could afford to own her by myself but choose not to as I would only take her out a couple of times a season. I own one sixth of it with a group of friends. That way, we each get a couple of weeks during the summer and we share the cost of purchase, maintenance, insurance, and hiring a captain. If I do it this way, it makes sense for me to own a boat. Many people buy a large purchase item that they don't use very much and then regret the money they spent or, even worse, have payments that long outlast the enjoyment they have. There's an old saying that, 'The two best days of a boater's life are the day they get their boat and the day they sell their boat.'"

"That's a very interesting way to buy something," admired Sarah.

"Yes, it is," Zane replied. "People are also jointly purchasing things like airplanes."

He motioned for them to sit down as the captain opened it up and the boat pounded through the large waves on the St Lawrence. After a short while, the captain slowed the boat down, and they cruised along enjoying the view and each other's company.

"How is your list making and the ultimate scenario letter writing coming?" Zane asked.

David spoke first, "We got it done last Saturday night and Sunday. We were so pumped to get it done, we could barely sleep."

"I thought you might have that problem," Zane smiled, "I know I did."

"Yeah," Sarah said. "It was invigorating. I just let my brain go and imagined what could be."

"That's great," Zane said. "I knew you would get it done quickly."

David spoke up shyly, "You know Zane, one of my dreams since I was a little kid was to sleep on a boat. I wrote it on my bucket list."

"I didn't know that," Zane said. "Tell me more."

David explained how he had put about eighty items on his bucket list and thought most of them were pipe dreams. Yet now, less than a week later, he can highlight one of the items already. "It's amazing."

"It's amazing how when you focus on something, it comes to fruition," said Zane.

Just than a freak rain shower poured down on them, and the three ran for cover under the canopy.

"Let's go down in the cabin as it's beginning to get dark. I have one short lesson for you before we call it a night, if you are interested."

"We sure are," Sarah said as she reached for her journal.

Snuggled inside, the three sat around the dinner table to discuss the next lesson.

Zane began by saying, "There are many different ways to invest the extra money you've earmarked for investment. Some we won't be able to invest in until you have larger sums of money."

"How do we get to that point?" David asked.

"You'll get there," Zane replied. "It may take a few years, but you'll get there. You're doing things right so far. All you have to do is keep following instructions and working hard."

"That's all?" Sarah asked hopefully.

"Yes, that's all," Zane replied. "Follow the formula others have used before you, and you can do it. It's like baking bread. Others have done it before you, so all you need to do is follow the recipe. Now, how many types of bread are there?"

David spoke up at this point because if it had to do with food he was there. "I'd say there are at least a hundred types of bread."

"Okay," Zane said, "you're probably right. Do you think the main ingredients change much?"

"I guess not," David said. "They will mostly have some sort of flour, salt, yeast, and maybe a sweetener like honey or sugar for the yeast to feed on."

"You're exactly right," Zane said. "It's the same with making money through investments; the main ingredients are the same, and there are hundreds of variations in what you can invest in."

"Okay, I think I'm getting it," Sarah said. "There are many different ways to go about it."

"Ok, good," Zane continued. "Today I'm not going to give you the actual things to invest in, only the main ingredients that you can apply to investing in general. The first ingredient is to diversify your portfolio."

As David wrote this in his journal, he said, "That's not a new one. Sarah's dad had been explaining about diversifying his stock portfolio forever."

"Correct," Zane said. "Nothing I will say is new. It's all time tested and true. Have you ever heard the saying, 'Don't put all your eggs in one basket'?"

"Yes," Sarah spoke up as she raised her eyes off the page of her journal for a moment.

"Well that's exactly what most people do. They put all their investments in the stock market, and because they have several different stocks and mutual funds, diversified all within one basket, the stock market, so that when the stock market falls, all you have is a basket full of scrambled eggs. Many people saw this happen to the diversified stock portfolio in 2008 and 2009. They were diversified but when the whole market went down 30% in one year, it was difficult to come out on top of that. I had a significant amount in the stock market in 2007, and I took 95% of it out and put it into other investments when the market started to fall. It continued to fall a total of 50% over the next two years. If I would have stayed with it, I would have lost 50% of my stock and mutual value. Do you know how much of the percentage gain I would have needed to make it back?"

"Fifty percent growth," David guessed.

"Wrong," said Zane, making a buzzer sound like he got the wrong answer on a game show. "It would take a 100% gain to break even, and if I was averaging, say, 12% per year return from then on, using the rule of 72, it would take six years to get back to even. So for two years, it went down and six years back up, for a total of eight years just to break even. Not a very good investment, right?"

"That's right," Sarah agreed. "Not a very good investment."

Zane made a buzzer sound again. "You can't win on every investment, but you should win on most. That's why if all your money was in the stock market through stocks, mutuals, and bonds, you aren't diversifying."

"What else is there to invest in?" David asked.

"Lots of things," Zane said. "We just aren't going to get into them tonight. Remember, we are only looking at the main ingredients. So it's not bad to be in the stock market. Just don't put all your wealth there."

"When I was young, my parents said don't put money in the stock market unless you can afford to lose it," offered Sarah.

Zane continued, "That was good advice. In the 1970's, a new product was birthed called a mutual fund. This was widely accepted as a safe investment when all it was was a group of people pooling their funds and mutually buying stocks that a management/research firm suggested. Thus the name mutual fund. The idea was that for a fee, a mutual fund manager would be able to pick the best stocks and help investors win. The trouble is that most managed mutuals don't even out perform the S & P 500 stock index after they take their management fees."

"I see," said Sarah.

"Another common thing taught about investments is, 'The higher the return, the higher the risk.' This is just not true. There are investments that typically offer a high rate of return with very low risk."

"Really?" asked David incredulously.

"Really," replied Zane. "That was another marketing tool. Sure it's true for things like a savings account at 0.5% low return and low risk, compared to stocks with a possible high return and possibly high risk. There are high return, low risk investments out there that you can find. Some require more money and a longer time frame for the investment. In other words, the investment is not very liquid like the stock market is. So, you should not put money in these types of investments that you may need to withdraw in an emergency, or to take advantage of another opportunity. That is what high investment savings accounts, an oxymoron like jumbo shrimp, and the stock market are good for. Be careful with the stock market though because if you have to get your money right away, it could be at a low cycle, and you'll lose money to sell at that time.

"The second ingredient is if you are going to make stocks or mutual funds part of your portfolio, you need to buy automatically each month or week so that you can take advantage of dollar cost averaging. That's a fancy word for buy more when they are on sale and fewer when they are expensive."

"I still don't get it," David said with a puzzled look on his face.

Zane continued, "It's like this example." He pulled out a piece of paper. "Let's say a stock, for the sake of ease, starts at $10.00 per share, and you are putting $100 per paycheck into the stock. With your first paycheck, you would buy 10 stocks."

"Got it," said Sarah.

Zane smiled. "Now, let's say the stock goes up to $20. Then you would only buy 5 stocks at this price."

"Shame they are going up," observed David.

"That's the problem, David," Zane agreed, nodding his head. "Most people buy when the price is high."

"What do you mean?" Sarah asked.

"Well," Zane continued, "most people buy their stocks or mutual funds during RRSP season. This causes a higher demand for stock and mutual funds, which then pushes the prices higher, so most people buy at the top of the market."

"Okay, I get it," David said. "I used to rush out and buy RRSP's in February to try to reduce my taxes. I even used to borrow money to do it."

"That's a mistake," Zane said, "and the interest on RRSP loans is not tax deductible. Effectively, the interest counters some or all of the gain of your investment purchase, especially since you are buying when the demand is high and paying the interest with after tax dollars."

"Right, I won't do that ever again," David said. "Gosh, Zane, you are incredible. We would be nowhere without you. I'd still be making so many mistakes!"

"We'd both be still making mistakes," corrected Sarah, patting David on the arm.

Zane smiled at the couple. "Don't feel bad. Mutual fund companies and banks spend millions of dollars in marketing to snare unsuspecting investors. Let's continue with my example. The next paycheck, the stock goes down to $10 and you buy 10 shares with your $100. The next paycheck, the shares go down to $5, and so your $100 bought 20 stocks."

"This is a much better scenario," said David.

"That's right," encouraged Zane. "You are buying more because the stocks are on sale. The next week they go back to 10 dollars, and you buy 10 shares with your $100. Now, five weeks have gone by and the stock is back where it started at $10. Let's see how much money you have made."

"It should be zero, should it not?" guessed Sarah.

Zane gleefully made that buzzer sounds again, which was starting to annoy Sarah. He smiled at her and began to draw the numbers out like this:

	Investment	Cost	Shares Purchase
Week 1	100	10	10
Week 2	100	20	5
Week 3	100	10	10
Week 4	100	5	20
Week 5	100	10	10
	500		55

55 x $10 = $550

David could not contain himself. "Are you telling me that the stock started at $10 and ended at $10, and I paid $500 in total, and now it's worth $550, a 10% gain, simply because I invested every week?"

"That's exactly it," Zane exclaimed happily. "That is the power of dollar cost averaging. If the stock was at say $11 after the five weeks, the gain would even be higher."

"That is so cool," David said. "So the money I have coming off my pay each week buying stocks in Coke is taking advantage of dollar cost averaging?"

"Correct," Zane responded. "And on top of it, your company matches a contribution amount to yours each week, don't they?"

"Yes they do," David replied. "You've got to be dumb not to take advantage of such a good deal once you understand it."

"Yes you do," Zane smiled. "Or up in debt to your eyeballs so that you can't take advantage of such a great program. Remember debt is the number one reason, in my opinion, why some people do not take advantage of opportunity when it comes their way. Fear combined with lack of knowledge would be a close second."

"This is so good to know, Zane," gasped Sarah as she shook the cramp out of her hand. "I might fill up this journal today! What's the third ingredient?"

"Let time do the heavy lifting."

Now it was Sarah's turn to look puzzled. Zane smiled again and continued. "Invest early and let time be your friend to do the heavy lifting. Let's look at twin brothers to see the difference time can make. Let's say in this example that both have found good investments at 12%.

The first brother is Bob. Bob decides that he is going to invest the $10,000 he made tree planting in the summer. His twin brother Jim decides to buy a new car and put his $10,000 as a downpayment because he can afford it, since he had a student loan for much more than he needs to go to school. Bob also goes to school with the loan but borrows less money. They are both 20 years old. Bob gets out of school and immediately pays back the loan when the interest was about to start since he had no car payment, insurance or maintenance. Jim on the other hand took 10 years to pay back the loan. When it was finished, he decided that his brother might have been smart, so he decides to put the $2,000 he was paying on his loans into an investment for the next few years. They went to school, by the way, for 5 years in engineering. Now see what happens as Jim starts to invest $2,000/year from age 32 on:

Bob 12%			Jim 12%		
Age	Investment	Value	Age	Investment	Value
20	10, 000	10,000	20	0	
26	10, 000	19, 738	26	0	

32	10, 000	38, 959	32		Starts Investing
38	10, 000	76, 900	38	12,000	16, 203
44	10, 000	151, 786	44	24,000	48, 266
50	10, 000	299, 599	50	36,000	111, 499
56	10, 000	591, 356	56	48,000	236, 310
62	10, 000	1, 167, 231	62	60,000	482, 665

You see, they both decided to retire at age 62. Bob invested a total of $10,000 and has $1, 167, 231 of growth. Jim invested $60,000 and has $482, 665. Jim invested six times as much as his brother Bob, and yet Bob had more than two times as much money in his investment. This is what I mean by let time do the heavy lifting."

"That's incredible!" Sarah said.

"It sure is," Zane said. "Particularly since a few choices when you are young can change the shape of your future. That's why I love to work with young couples like yourself. You have time on your side. That's not to say if you were older, I would not be able to help you. It just means it may be harder."

"Is there a fourth ingredient in the bread we are making?"

All three started chuckling as they got the pun Sarah unknowingly had just said. David started to laugh as he said, "Let's make the dough and let time let it rise."

"That's really funny," Zane chuckled. "I think I'll use it next time in my analogy. I'll be sure to add the fact that the yeast not only needs time, but warmth, and that the higher the warmth, or rate of return, the faster the dough rises and the investment grows. I love it," said Zane.

David spoke first after they had finished laughing. "Zane you said you would use this the next time you teach this. Do you teach others the same thing?"

"Do you remember what you told me after you changed the tire?"

"Sure," said David. "Just to do something nice for someone else or pass on the good deed. It's what my dad taught me."

"Exactly," Zane said. " Your dad was bang on and so was mine. He taught me the same thing. So when my mentors, mostly books, taught me about building wealth, it was only natural for me to want to share my knowledge and success with others, just as I'm sure you will as well. It's like when you find a great restaurant. Do you keep it a secret in fear you won't be able to get a table next time you go, or do you tell your friends so they can also enjoy it?"

"I'd tell my friends," David replied easily.

"Exactly, and I'll do the same with the investments I've found. There is no guarantee that the food or service will be as good for your friends, just like the investment may not perform as well, but past performance is one of the best indications we have of future performance.

"Now onto the fourth ingredient. Don't invest in anything you do not understand. When you buy a stock or a mutual fund, you are buying a piece of the company, or companies as in the case with the mutual. You better know what you are investing in and understand it. That or keep your money because you are just taking a stab in the dark otherwise. I'm not saying you need to know everything about it, but a general understanding is necessary. You don't know how many people invest in mutuals which have companies within them that they would never have invested in otherwise."

"What do you mean, Zane?"

"Well, some people are for instance admittedly against stem cell experimental research on unborn infants' brain stem cells because of the ways these cells are harvested. They then are horrified to find bio research companies in their mutual portfolio that practice this. They had no clue that they owned a piece of a company that does this practice."

"I see," said Sarah with a tear in her eye.

Zane could see he touched a nerve, so he quickly moved on. "The last thing to understand is that these truths about money, debt, giving or charity, investing, and thankfulness are universal laws just like gravity or centrifugal force, momentum etc. Let's use gravity for instance. Whether you believe in it or not, it still exists. If you step off the top stair of the entrance to this cabin, you'll go down to the next step. You aren't going to float up in the air. Even if you don't believe gravity exists, it still applies its force on you. Money principals are also universal, and the effects of going against them can be almost as devastating as stepping off a tall building thinking you are not going to fall. Money problems have caused marriages to break up, people to commit suicide, huge stress to the breaking point of people losing their health, and homelessness."

"Wow," said Sarah, "you really know how to cheer a girl up."

"I know," said Zane. "It's a gift I have. It's important that you know my passion about this subject is not about a love of money, it's not about money mastering me, but about me mastering money. It takes passion in life to accomplish any great thing. By the way," he said leaning back on his seat. "you can take the word passion and break it down. It means 'Pass I On.' In other words, you'll pass yourself on to others, and it's contagious. People will circle around and support someone who has passion in an area they believe in."

"This is getting really deep," observed David.

"You're right," replied Zane. "I get really fired up about the things I'm passionate about. While we are on the topic of definitions, I think it is important that you know my thoughts on my definition of wealth. People can be wealthy without being rich. True wealth comes when we are content with what we have, ambitious to learn and earn more and we are living under our means so that there is money for giving and wealth building and no pressure from consumer debt."

"Your passion shows and that is a great definition for what it is to be wealthy, Zane," Sarah encouraged.

"I know, I just want you to catch the passion and pass it on. Not for the sake of what money can buy but for the good money can do. People who are broke by choice, i.e. consumer debt, are unable to help those people in desperate need. People with money and no debt are in the best position to help. I've found that most of my rich friends give way more to charity than my poorer friends."

"That makes sense," Sarah continued to encourage him.

"The last ingredient I'm going to talk about tonight is your share of influence. Then we'll need to get to bed as tomorrow is a big lesson and you'll have lots to learn."

"Are you going to cruise all night?" David asked.

"No, we're going to be anchoring shortly. It's not safe to travel at night."

"I see," said David.

Zane continued, "The last ingredient is your average income. Interestingly enough, this is almost always about the average of the income of your six closest friends."

"Are you saying I have to change my friends?" asked David.

"Not necessarily. You may be close to them for a season and then later decide to find or simply migrate to new friends who have similar interests in wealth building. Some may be inspired by you and follow along, and others may just stop calling because they are uncomfortable with the changes they see in you. There are very few true friends that a person retains for a life time. When you get one of those you will know it."

"How?" Sarah asked.

Zane smiled, "Once I started to build wealth, some of my friends rejoiced with me, some were jealous and bitter, and others wanted handouts. A very few actually wanted to learn from me."

"I see," said David. "I've noticed that some of my friends don't call much anymore since I've changed my spending ways and don't eat out and party as much."

"So true," Zane continued. "Some friends will love you no matter what, and you them likewise. They mourn when you mourn, and most importantly, they celebrate your successes. A true friend stays through thick and thin. It's a connection almost like a lifelong marriage."

"I see," said Sarah. "That type of friendship is worth its weight in gold."

"It definitely is," Zane replied with a yawn. "I guess it's bed time. You guys take the front cabin. The washroom is on your left. Feel free to have a shower in the morning. We have plenty of water and sanitation on board.

Just remember the hot water tank is small, so if you shower too long, you'll be rinsing in cold water."

"Okay, thanks for today," Sarah replied.

The three said their good nights and headed off to bed. David was the first to fall unconscious as the gentle rocking of the boat lulled him to sleep. Sarah was exhausted from all the learning and was not far behind David in drifting into a deep sleep.

<u>Friday</u>

We are on a 38 foot cruise boat on the St. Lawrence with Zane! It's such a beautiful evening!!! He invited us for the night and we were glad to accept. One of David's Bucket List items has already come true, and it has only been less than a week since he wrote it out. He gets to sleep on a boat... So glad we get to spend this time with Zane!

His Advice:
- Investing is like baking bread. There are a few main ingredients or principles to invest in
- 1: Diversification – being diversified in the stock market only is like having different kind of eggs in the same basket
  - Fallacy: " The higher the return, the higher the risk" – some high return investments have low risk. Often these aren't liquid like the stock market and

can't be withdrawn in case
of emergency
- 2: Buy automatically each
month. You buy every week
or month, so you buy more
when on sale and less when
expensive. A good way to take
advantage of volatility using
dollar cost averaging.
  - *Don't buy RRSP's in Feb
  to reduce taxes - will pay
  too much
  - Debt = #1 reason why
  people don't see or are
  unable to take advantage
  of opportunities. Fear and
  lack of knowledge is a
  close #2.
- 3. Let time do the heavy
lifting - Start investing early
as the power of compound
return over time is amazing.
- 4. Invest in what you
understand - you are a part
owner
- Universal truths about money,
debt, giving, investing, and
thankfulness.
  - *People with money and
  no debt are in the best
  position to help others in
  need. Rich people are able

to give much more than
the poor.
- * My income = average
income of my six closest
friends. Choose friends
wisely!!

MY DECISIONS AND ACTION ITEMS

Look into what I can invest in regularly and automatically.

Is there any investments I have that I do not understand?

What changes should I make to my investment portfolio?

Is my current investment advisor the best one for me?

What investments do I want to learn/investigate?

SIXTH GEAR

Morning came before they knew it. David awoke to the smell of freshly ground and brewed coffee. He gave Sarah a few gentle kisses on her nose, and she started to stir. The smell of coffee hit her nostrils, and for a split second, she didn't have a clue as to where she was. The recollection hit as the gentle rocking of the bed came back to her.

"What time is it," Sarah asked.

"I think about 8:00 a.m.," he responded.

"Oh my!" Sarah exclaimed. "That means Zane has been up for 2 ½ hours."

"That's okay," David replied as he leant down to kiss her more passionately.

"No way!" Sarah exclaimed as she jumped out of bed. "These walls are paper thin!"

"Fine," David groaned as be acknowledged defeat and rolled out of bed.

As the couple surfaced to meet the day, Zane greeted them with a chirpiness that the freshly woken couple really were not ready for. "Did you sleep well?"

"So good," Sarah murmured sleepily. She glanced at her watch and recoiled in shock. They had been sleeping for over ten hours.

"That was the best sleep I think I've ever had," David replied as he reached back to hold his lower back with both hands. Surprised, he realized his back did not hurt this morning. He helped himself to a cup of coffee. "Most mornings it takes my back a couple of hours to loosen up after sleeping. Today I feel perfect. That bed was super comfortable."

"Thanks for noticing," was Zane's reply. "I believe in getting the best mattress around and getting a new one every five to ten years, depending on use."

"Why is that?" inquired Sarah.

"There are two reasons," Zane answered. "The first is we tend to spend one third of our life in bed. I think it should be the most comfortable time as possible. I'm not saying you should spend one third of your money on your bed and bedroom, although it's usually the most overlooked room in the house. The bed may sag, the furniture is old, dresser drawers don't open properly, and often the bedroom becomes the place we collect things. One's bedroom needs to be a calming sanctuary so you can de-stress from a hard day. No TV and no clutter."

"No TV? I think everyone I know has a TV in their bedroom."

"I read a survey once that said couples with a messy bedroom and a TV in it had almost half as much romance as couples with a clutter free, TV free master bedroom."

"I'm up for cleaning as soon as we get home," David said smiling and winking at Sarah.

"What's the second reason, Zane?"

"The second reason is that after a great night's sleep, I'm able to be my best for work, family, and friends. My mind works better, I'm more creative, and believe it or not, I make more money."

"Those are all great reasons," Sarah replied.

"Enough talk," Zane said. "You guys must be starving. I've prepared a great breakfast for you. We have grapefruit, oatmeal, boiled eggs, whole grain toast, and coffee."

"Looks great," David said. "I could eat a horse."

"Fortunately, I don't have one of those," Zane chuckled.

After breakfast Zane requested them to change into a bathing suit and to bring up their journals. He would meet them up on the sun deck. He had arranged three round chairs facing the sun, and the captain was cruising west at a nice slow pace. Sarah and David started to get their sea legs and barely noticed the gentle rocking and up and down motion of the boat as it climbed and descended the swells on the St. Lawrence.

Zane started talking in a very enthusiastic manner. "This is my favourite gear. Sixth gear you can do so much in."

"We're ready," David said eagerly.

"I know you are," Zane replied. "Otherwise, we wouldn't be here."

With pen in hand, Sarah and David waited to take notes.

"First of all," Zane continued, "I need to congratulate you for making it this far. Many do implement the first lessons, and then they are needing or wanting all the lessons. But they aren't mentally or financially ready. It would be like trying to start your car from a stop in sixth gear. You are going to stall the engine. The same thing happens if you don't do the first steps I've prescribed. Your engine will fail, and you'll blame the information, not that you started in the wrong place.

"The first step was to FACE reality, recognize where you are at and that things have to change. The second was tracking your spending and working within a budget that includes saving and giving, and doing a regular net worth statement. Next one, you had a cushion and refused to spend on credit. You knock out your debt starting smallest one first and so on, remembering to celebrate the victories as you become consumer debt free. This includes owing nothing on vehicles. We learned about getting proper insurance and building a team of professionals around you like a lawyer, doctor, accountant, real estate agent, insurance broker, mortgage broker and life insurance broker and getting a will, living will and power of attorney. Finally, we learned to increase our cushion to 3-6 months and then increase our giving and wealth building savings to 10% of our gross income and save 5% for large purchases and maintenance."

Sarah and David were nodding enthusiastically. David was a little emotional realizing how far they had come. He gripped his coffee and choked back tears. "Thanks so much, Zane. We've come so far. Life is more fun and the financial stress in our lives has been eliminated. Our net worth has gone from in the negatives to $100,000, and we have a closer marriage because we are walking this road together."

"I'm glad you're pleased," Zane replied kindly, "but I'd be remiss if I didn't give you the next two pieces to the puzzle. Remember I said you shouldn't invest in anything you don't understand? Well another principal is to spend at least one hour a week looking at your financial wealth portfolio and examining future investment options. I'm going to give you lots of investment options to review and learn about, and then in a year or two or three, you'll be ready to make your first investment."

David looked surprised. "Do I really have to spend a year or more gaining enough knowledge to make an educated investment? I thought I'd be ready next month."

"No, I am not saying that. It might, but it's more likely that it'll take you that long to save up enough money to invest in one of the great investment tools I am suggesting."

"Do you mean they have a minimum threshold?" Sarah asked.

"Yes, that's right," Zane answered. "Not only do some of them require you to have a minimum investment, some of these investments are restricted to what type of investor can invest."

"Are you saying that some companies are not wanting everyone's money?" David questioned.

"No, not that. It's the government that regulates who can invest, and it's different in each province as it's provincially regulated. I'll get into all that a little later this afternoon. Right now, you need to know what to do with the extra money you're saving. There are many possibilities for it, and it's important to know that the faster you can put money away, the faster it'll start to work for you. The government has a few programs that you can take advantage of to expedite your success."

David and Sarah gave Zane a look that made him laugh.

"You may find it hard to believe, but the government really does want you to succeed financially and be ready for retirement."

"I guess that way they don't have to look after you when you are old or bankrupt," David chuckled.

"One program the government has given Canadians is a tax free savings account, also called a TFSA. Most people didn't care when the government brought it out because they didn't see the power of it. Right now, the maximum you can put in is $5,000 per year. You can take the money out at any time and can put it back in the following year. Your contribution room grows each year by $5,000, whether you've registered or not, and you each can have an account. That is $10,000 per couple per year. If you each started putting $5,000 away in 2009, by 2012 you could each have $20,000 in contributions in the program. You can also catch up at any time. So if you stopped putting money in after just the first year, in 2012 you could each put in $15,000. The next year after using up your room, you can each then put $5,000 in again. Most people think because it is called a tax free savings account that it is just for a savings account, and with interest being at about 0.5% right now, they're saying 'thanks a lot and no thanks.'

Sarah snorted, "Sounds like what I'd say. Even a bond pays more interest."

Zane continued, "You can treat your TFSA like an RRSP and have regular installments put in it every week or every month in a mutual or stock, as long as you're in a self directed RRSP, TFSA or RESP plan with your financial advisor."

"Does this mean you can use dollar cost averaging on these account as well and what is an RESP account?" David asked, understanding more quickly than Sarah.

"It sure does," Zane replied, "and the beauty is, unlike an RRSP where you will pay tax on both the contribution and growth of your investments when you remove it, a TFSA account is able to hold the same type of investments as your RRSP, and because you don't get a tax deduction when you contribute, when you withdrawal from the TFSA, both your contribution and the growth of the investment is tax free. The RESP we will discuss later. It is a program for saving for your children's education and I don't think you have any children yet unless there is something that you want to tell me."

No… Nothing to tell yet," Sarah sheepishly replied.

David started to get excited and sat a little further ahead in his chair to take notes. He had forgotten he was on a boat, being so intent on listening to Zane. "Okay, let's see if I get it. These other types of investments you have been talking about can also be bought within a TFSA. The TFSA has the potential to be a tax free retirement plan. I'm not sure the government knew how powerful a tool they've given Canadians because unlike RRSP's, which grow tax free until you remove money and are hit with a tax bill on every dollar you remove, the TFSA is funded with after tax dollars. The growth is tax free, and when you take your money or growth out, it's totally tax free. With the power of compounding rate of return, this is a no brainer for everyone's wealth building portfolio."

"Exactly," Zane said. "Let's look at what this money would be worth in say 40 years." As Zane was talking, he pulled out his iPhone. "I just love this app. It's a financial calculator that simulates the HP106II financial calculator. If you decide to put in the $10,000 total as a couple each year and we are able to make a return of say 8%, at the end of 40 years you would have $2, 590, 565 tax free dollars. If you had an investment where it went in monthly, you could have even more!"

"I think I get it," said Sarah. "I'd heard about the TFSA before, but it was just financial jargon in my mind. Now I'm starting to see how powerful it can be."

"Right," said Zane, "and that's why it's important to learn about financial options and investment opportunities for at least an hour a week; otherwise when a great opportunity crosses your path, you may either not be looking for it or not see it or understand it even if you are looking."

"Huh," Sarah mused. "So do we put all our extra money in a TFSA?"

"No, I would not necessarily put it there initially. The fees to open an account self-directed are a little expensive for $5,000 just yet."

"Then where do we put it?" David asked.

Zane smiled, "I'd suggest you put it against your mortgage initially. Let's pay that down as fast as possible."

"Even if rates are low right now?"

"Yes," Zane replied. "Especially if you were just going to put the TFSA into an interest bearing account that only makes say 0.5 to 1%. The TFSA is a great place to keep most of your emergency fund. Since you didn't contribute in previous years, you each have room for $20,000. That's a total of $40,000, which is great because interest is at the highest tax rate."

"Okay, now you've lost me," Sarah spoke up.

"It's like this," Zane explained, "you remember how you have different tax levels for different income levels?"

"Yes," Sarah replied.

"Well, interest is taxed at your highest tax bracket whether you take it out of the bank or not. As soon as it is made it is taxable the next tax return time. Now, things like dividends on stocks have a preferential tax rate, which is about half the maximum rate, and the tax is due after the dividend is issued. Capital Gains Tax occurs when something you own grows in value and you sell it. Capital Gains Tax is at 50% of your highest tax rate and isn't due until you sell the investment, and then it's due on the next tax return. RRSP's are a temporary shelter from the tax, so interest and dividend shares are nested here. Growth investments grow tax free until you sell them and then have a 50% reduction, so an RRSP may not be the best place to keep these as you will be taxed at full rate when you remove from the account at tax time. Since your TFSA is permanently tax free, you can keep any type of investment in it, but an interest type investment is the best kept in the TFSA. There are maximums to capital gains allowances and you will want to check with your accountant on tax strategies going forward. We want to pay our required taxes as they support many great things and yet no point in paying more than the government requires us to. Your RESP can be in any allowable investment as the tax strategy on removal is that the growth is taxed in your child's hand and they will most likely pay no tax since they are a student.""This all sounds very complicated," David said, shaking his head. "And I thought you said not to invest in interest as it was too low at around half a percent."

"Yes, that is right," Zane replied. "An interest bearing account is too low and yet there are mortgages you could invest in that would return 8 to 10%. That amount of interest is great when it is in a tax free account. That's why I recommended that you have a great tax accountant, financial planner, and lawyer. You need to have a basis of knowledge as well though, so you can ask the right questions and know that they, your financial specialists, are guiding you properly.

"Now back to the mortgage pay down. Let's say your mortgage is at 5%. That's a guaranteed 5% return on your investment when you put money there, because any money you save paying the bank is like money earned. And it's tax free savings because you would have to pay the interest with after tax dollars. Are you following me?"

"We sure are," David and Sarah replied.

Zane loved the fact that David and Sarah were not afraid to ask a questions and risk looking ignorant. He had once heard the saying: 'It is better to ask a question and look ignorant for a minute, than not ask the question and be ignorant for a lifetime.' He went on. "Now the reason we're paying down our mortgage is so that in the future, we can leverage your home to buy other investments."

"What do you mean leverage our home?" Sarah asked with a little hesitation.

Zane took out a piece of paper. In the middle of the page, he drew a large rock. "If I was to move the big rock, I could use a strong board and a small rock as a fulcrum to leverage my weight, as long as the board is longer from the little rock to me than the board is long from the little rock to the big rock. I will have leverage and be able to move the big rock more easily."

"I understand what leverage is," Sarah said a little indignantly. "What do you mean leverage my home? Isn't the goal to pay off the mortgage and be totally debt free?"

"Totally debt free is very nice and cozy," Zane said, "but it may not be the wisest place to put all that money. Your home is generally over time going to increase in value, whether it has a mortgage on it or not."

"Right," said David.

"Well," Zane continued, "when you first bought your home with a down payment, no matter how much you paid, you've already leveraged your home if it has a mortgage on it."

Both Sarah and David looked puzzled again.

"Let me explain. Let's say a person buys a house for $300,000 with 20% down. That means he or she bought a house with $60,000 of her own money or effort and $240,000 of the mortgag**ee**'s money. So she leveraged someone else's money to buy the house."

"That's right," David replied.

Zane drew another one of his diagrams.

60,000   (House) 300,000

240,000

Bank Mortgage

"Now, lets say that in a year that property went up 6%. That would be $18,000 in growth right? $300,000 x 0.06 = 18,000."

"Right," Sarah agreed.

Zane pulled out his phone again. "The interest on the $240,000 mortgage at 5% with a 25 year amortization is about $11,880, give or take a little, depending on whether the mortgage is in the USA or Canada. Mortgage interest is stated a little differently in the two countries. So, if our house increased in value by $18,000 and we paid $11,880 in interest, our net gain is $18,000-11,880, which equals $6,120. If we divide by our initial downpayment of $60,000, we will find our rate of return, which is 10.2%. You see, although we got a 6% increase on our home, we got a 10.2% increase on our down payment. This is the power of leverage if done properly."

"So most people start with their house leveraged?" asked Sarah.

"Exactly!" Zane was getting excited again. "Paying down the mortgage means we keep more of the growth and less goes to interest, but we are not leveraging as much, which in itself is safe and not a bad thing and yet if interest rates are lower than the rate of growth of the house price having less leverage decreases our rate of return on our initial investment."

Sarah spoke up again, "But Zane, my dad taught me to pay off the mortgage as fast as possible and to never borrow against the house to invest."

"I would agree," Zane answered, "if the investment was too risky or you didn't have enough money in reserve. You want to have a year of emergency fund money in case things do go a little wrong. It is funny, even the government has rules and regulations to make it difficult for financial coaches to recommend to leverage your homes for investment purposes, and yet people increase their mortgages all the time and roll in a whole whack of consumer debt. Then they start buying all over again. This consumerism eats up the growth equity they have in their home, and many people feel good about this debt level because they only have a mortgage. Hello, people! You still have consumer debt; it's just disguised as a mortgage."

"Huh," said David.

Zane continued at an even faster pace. "If we use the net worth statement as the litmus test, when we leverage our home for consumerism, the net worth stays the same over time. When we leverage for investment, we have an investment that counter balances the debt on the mortgage. That investment is most likely going to go up over time, so in the end our net worth statement will be much higher then the person who rolled consumer debt into their mortgage."

"Makes sense when you put it that way," Sarah admitted.

"Also," Zane continued, "I wouldn't leverage a home more than I can comfortably pay the payment on and once again, only if the investment wasn't risky. Oh by the way, the interest you pay on the leveraged part that's invested is tax deductible on your income tax, as long as it's not invested in an RRSP.

"Okay, enough about leveraging for now, although we will revisit it in the future as I'm so excited about how with leveraging you could buy 64 rental properties in the 40 years before you retire and not have to put any more downpayment money than most would already have in equity in their home."

"Are you serious?" quizzed David.

"Very serious," said Zane. "It is one of the ways I have amassed my portfolio of Real Estate. Get your pens ready because I will give you the different types of investments and a brief explanation of each.

"First, there is a REIT, or Real Estate Investment Trust. This is a trust fund of money that the REIT managers buy real estate with. Frequently, it's apartment buildings worth millions of dollars that investors wouldn't be able to buy on their own. These large buildings tend to have better returns and cash flow than you could get by buying a single unit or a duplex etc. Your investment value goes up each year as well, as the real estate appreciates and you generally get a monthly cheque based on the profitability or cash flow of the portfolio.

"The second is land banking. Some of the greatest wealth has been accumulated by developing raw land. There are companies that buy raw land in growth areas and then work with the city to rezone and build a development plan so that builders will want to buy the land. Let's say a land banking company starts buying land at say $3000 an acre. They then put about $1000 an acre into rezoning and master planning and then wait anywhere from 3 to 10 years for the land to be ready to be built on. The builder/developer will pay over $30,000 an acre, put roads on it, and build houses where a lot will sell for say $90,000 and the builder can get say 4 to 6 lots out of an acre.

"If a developer can make so much money, why do they want investors?" David asked.

"That's a good question," Zane smiled back. "The land banker cannot land bank more land because all their money is tied up, so to take advantage of more opportunity, they're willing to share some of the spoils with investors. One of the ones I am invested with has been averaging about 14% over the last several years and no one has ever lost any money."

"That's awesome," Sarah exclaimed.

"It sure is," Zane replied. "Remember though, a lot of these investments in Ontario are limited to investors who are either high income earners, or who have lots of assets, or who are investing $150,000 in the investment. This is not their whole investment portfolio. And once again, it's different in every province and state."

"Sounds a little complicated," David noted.

"It is," Zane replied, "but spend a couple of hours with your investment professional and they can explain if you qualify. I have also bought properties in developing areas like Belize and Costa Rica for fun and to diversify. Buying property in depressed markets in the USA is another opportunity I am looking into.

"Another interesting investment I made was in a commercial land development near Calgary. I used RRSP money because the way the investment was structured, it made the most sense. With this investment I bought a $100,000 bond inside my RRSP which was secured against the property. The bond paid out 6% per year non compounded at the end of 5 years. So in other words, the rate of return was 30% over 5 years. Not a great return but it's guaranteed, and the bond is registered against the property and is an RRSP product, and therefore tax sheltered with in my RRSP. The fun part was because I bought the bond, I was eligible to buy 1,000 shares in the company that owned the development land for $1,000 more. The land is sold off as it is developed; I'm a part owner and will share in the profits. This will come as dividends out side of my RRSP and will receive preferred tax treatment because it is a dividend.

"Bonds can be kind of fun but a little more risky sometimes. Solid bonds like Government Bonds are very secure, yet usually the return is quiet low. High yield bonds, or junk bonds as they are fondly called, sometimes have a higher yield or rate of return but are a higher risk depending on what companies or properties are behind the bond. This is how they work. Let's say a bond is issued at $100 a bond and are to return 12% per year and then be cashed in in say 10 years. Now, as long as the companies with the bond do well, you'll receive your 12% per year and your money back, but it isn't guaranteed. Now let's say the companies are going extremely well. You may be able to resell your bond for $120. The person buying the bond at $120 would receive still 12% of the original price. This means the new buyer is only getting a 10% rate of return, but he or she may be happy with that because the company or companies that back the bond are doing well, so the risk is reduced.

"Now, let's say the companies are not going well because the economy is not faring well or whatever. You decide you want to sell your $100 bond, concerned it might fail and that you'd lose your money. You decide to sell after several years of receiving 12% because you know the companies are only scraping by. The market dictates that you can get only $50 for your bond, but $50 is better than nothing. The person buying the bond takes a big risk, but if it works they will be receiving 12% on the original $100 bond or the equivalent of 24% per year on their $50 bond. Fun is it not?”

“Yes, very fun,” David agreed and yet still looked a little confused.

Zane continued at this fast pace, “Second mortgages, construction loans or MICS, Mortgage Investment Corporations, are other ways to earn 8-12%. These are great for RRSP and TFSA money.” He filled David’s coffee cup for the third time. “Now for one of my favourites. I just love real estate rentals. Either commercial or residential.”

“Why are real estate rentals your favourite?” Sarah asked. She helped herself to another half of a grapefruit and began meticulously cutting between the fruit and the skin.

“Well for one, it’s one thing that I am more personally involved in managing and overseeing. It can be more work or a royal pain in the butt if you let in the wrong tenant, but it also can be very rewarding. Let me explain how I can get great returns on this kind of product. First of all, you can leverage it.”

“Okay,” said Sarah smiling wryly as she took a bite of grapefruit. She picked up her pen, posed to write. “You don’t have to explain that again.”

“Good,” Zane grinned back. “I like thoughtful learners. Now, let’s say we want to buy a $400,000 triplex and we have $20,000 saved up. This is only 5% of the purchase price, and I want 20% down to get the best financing possible. I’ve also been paying down my mortgage on my principal residence so I can easily remortgage to remove $60,000. Now I have $80,000 down on the triplex and I’m double leveraged, so to speak. When I run the numbers on the unit, there is enough income from the three tenants to pay the expenses for the triplex, the mortgage payment on the triplex, and the payment on the extra $60,000 I removed from my personal house, with $50 per month left over. There are now three factors working in my favour to build wealth.”

“Really?” David chimed in. “I only see the one, which is leveraged growth on the property value.”

“That is one,” Zane responded, “but let’s look at the potential down the road. First of all, real estate in Ottawa has averaged a little over 6% growth per year, compounded for the last 40 years or so. I think it would be fair to use 5% as our standard. Okay, so our original cash unleveraged money for investment was $20,000. The triplex went up the first year at, say, 5%. So, 5% on $400,000 is 400,000x0.05, which equals $20,000."

David gaped at Zane.

Zane smiled. "That's right, David. Our original $20,000 made $20,000 in one year, which is a 100% rate of return in one year."

"That's incredible!" Sarah almost jumped off her seat with enthusiasm.

Zane held up his hand. "It gets even better," he continued. "Rent is allowed to go up by the cost of living index, so you would increase the rent every year. If you locked in your mortgage for 5 or 10 years, your cash flow will go up over time as rent increases. The third great thing is that the tenant is paying down your mortgage principle month after month, so the amount you owe is getting less on both mortgages. I also recommend using your own income to pay down your personal mortgage on your home. And get this, the interest on the 1st mortgage and the portion of your mortgage on your home along with your maintenance cost on the triplex are all tax deductible. Because of these factors, you would expect your rate of return to go up in the future years. Right?"

Sarah and David nodded as if in a trance. They couldn't believe these numbers.

"You're wrong!" Zane said gleefully. "Let's look at Year Two. The property is now worth $420,000, and we've paid down about $6,500 of the mortgage, so we now have $46,500 of equity in the property."

"How do you get that?" David asked.

"I am glad you are thinking now," Zane joked. "Here's the math."

      $420,000 (property value)
- $313,500 (mortgage)
- <u>$60,000</u> (mortgage on personal property assuming you paid
        nothing this year)
      $45,500 (equity)

"Oh I see it," David conceded.

"Great," Zane continued. "The next year, we get an increase of value of 5% again, which on $420,000 is a $21,000 gain. Now our equity is $46,500 so our growth is 21,000 divided by 46,500, which equals 45.16%. A 45% rate of return is still fantastic, although I would still not change anything yet. Now don't forget that rent has gone up and you have been paying down the $60,000 on your personal home when you've had money. Here we go with the numbers and assumptions again.

"Let's say the property is now worth $441,000, and the third year the property goes up 5% again, which would be about a $22,000 gain, rounded down for ease of number crunching. The property is now worth $463,000. Let's take a closer look at the equity considering how the rent went up and the personal cash flow you've been able to use to pay down the mortgage on your home by $10,000 over the last couple of years. Let's look at the rate of return."

Zane worked quickly on his iPhone app and found the mortgage balance after two years with a 5% interest rate and a 25 year amortization.

      $463,000 (property value)
   - $306,466 (1st mortgage)
   - <u>$50,000</u> (mortgage on home)
      $106,534 (equity)

$22,000 growth on $106,534 is about 20.65% return. Still not bad, eh? Now let's look at year four!"

"I can't imagine!" murmured Sarah.

"Property goes up 5% again, so about $23,000 rounding down for simplicity. The property is now worth $486,000."

      $486,000 (property value)
   - $299,175 (1st mortgage)
   - <u>$50,000</u> (line of credit) assuming you paid nothing this year
      $136,825 (equity)

"$136,825 equity divided by $23,000 of growth equals over a 16.8% rate of return. Still not bad, but not so amazing. After 5 years is when the magic starts, so let's keep going okay?"

"Don't stop now!" exclaimed David eagerly.

"Here we go, Year 5," Zane said with excitement in his voice. "The property is now worth $486,000, plus 5% growth, so $24,300, which makes it $510,300."

> $510,300 (property value)
> - $291,512 (1ˢᵗ mortgage)
> - $50,000 (mortgage on home) assuming you paid nothing this year for ease of calculation
> $168,788 (equity)

"$24,300 on $168,788 equals 14.4%. So the rate of return is 14%."

"That is still very good," David said, "but you said this is when it gets exciting?"

"It is," Zane replied. "Remember we put $20,000 of our money down and paid about $10,000 more on the mortgage on our home? We now after only five years have $168,788 in equity plus what was paid down in year five which was another 8,055 which gives us an equity of $176,843 and our rental income is higher then it was five years ago. The magic begins when we take out a new 80% mortgage on the $510,300, which would be about $408,000. Now, we owe about $283,456 on the first mortgage, so we have $124,544 extra money after we pay off the existing mortgage with the new 80% mortgage. This is enough to put 20% down on our next triplex, about a $500,000 value, pay the legal fees and land transfer tax and have a little left over to upgrade the older triplex. "Now, continue for 5 more years and we'll have about $250,000 plus to buy another two triplexes. Another five years, and you'll have over $500,000 in equity to remove from the triplexes to buy another four triplexes. What it works out to roughly is that in forty years, with a fair bit of effort and work with very little risk, you've turned your initial $20,000 and your $60,000 mortgage into over twelve million dollars of equity and you'll own 64 properties."

"Now that's almost unbelievable!" Sarah stuttered. "If I hadn't seen the numbers, I would never have believed it."

"Fascinating, isn't it?" Zane beamed.

David got serious now and leaned forward. "So you are telling me I need to pay down my mortgage, save $20,000 or so and make sure my emergency fund is fully funded, and then I can start something like this?"

"Yes, that's right," Zane nodded.

"I guess a key is having a great real estate agent," David said as he nudged Sarah.

"You're right," Zane replied. "A great real estate agent working for you under a buyer agency to find a great investment is invaluable, and they can most likely steer you in the direction of good plumbers, electricians, painters, flooring suppliers, mortgage brokers and any other professional you are going to need to make this happen smoothly. Some people prefer to start with a townhouse for their first investment as it is less expensive, requires less down payment and they are initially only dealing with one tenant"

Sarah looked puzzled for a moment and then formulated a question. "If you can turn $20,000 into a million in 20 years, why would you do the other investments you mentioned earlier? They don't have as good a rate of return."

"Now that is an excellent question," Zane answered. "First, I want other investments because then I am diversified if something happens to the real estate market. Secondly, being a landlord is work. The other types of investments are more passive in nature. I need to watch them, but I don't have to actively work at it."

"I have so many more questions," Sarah said.

"Good," Zane smiled, "and they'll have to wait. It's time to go get dressed for lunch as we're approaching Ivy Lee Inn. We'll be having lunch in their dining room."

Sarah squinted, "You didn't say I should bring clothes for a fancy dining room."

Zane reassured her that casual clothes were just fine. Most of the diners would also be boaters and so anything more than a bathing suit would be acceptable.

Lunch was superb, and shortly after 2:00 p.m. they were back on the boat and heading east for the return journey.

"Great," said Sarah, "now I can ask my questions."

"Not so fast," Zane responded. "All work and no play makes for a very boring trip. You guys get into your suits. Our captain has a little fun planned for us."

As Sarah and David were changing into their bathing suits, they could tell that the boat was traveling quiet a bit faster as it clammed into the waves it bounced them around a little. It was difficult to change, and at one point David found both his legs through the same leg whole in his trunks. They both giggled as David took one leg out and put it in the right hole. Once they were ready to head out of the cabin, they fell forward onto the bed as the captain cut the engines abruptly. David laughed with delight as Sarah had fallen on top of him. Sarah pushed herself up off the bed and laughed as she said, "Not this time, big boy."

David laughed to as he chased Sarah out of the cabin. Once back on deck, they noticed that they were in a sort of cove that protected them from the rough water. There were twenty foot rock walls around the cove. It was beautiful and peaceful.

Zane motioned for them to join him at the back of the boat where there was a swim platform and a ladder. The captain had secured the anchor.

"Follow me," Zane said as he dove into the dark water and disappeared for what seemed like minutes. Finally his head popped up half way to the rock bank.

"Now that we can see him, we can follow him," David said as he pushed Sarah into the water and did a cannon ball beside her just as she surfaced.

"You're such a kid," Sarah said to him as she splashed his face with water when he emerged and was trying to wipe water out of his eyes.

David closed his eyes and started swimming towards where Zane was headed. In no time Sarah was way ahead of him. "Okay, yeah, I forgot you were a swimming instructor and a life guard as a teenager!" David joked. "That's fine. Leave me behind. Hopefully I won't drown out here all alone."

Sarah laughed wickedly and motored ahead.

Zane waited on shore for the two to arrive. He grabbed a rope leading to a tree at the top of the incline and started climbing. "Use this," he said, "to help steady yourself as you climb up the cliff. It's a little steep."

Sarah looked at him a little doubtfully. "I'll go first," David offered with a smile.

"Oh Zane! This is so worth it! The view is beautiful!" Sarah called out as she made her way up.

"Sarah! Wait until you see it up here!" David huffed from his view at the top.

"It sure is," Zane exclaimed, giving Sarah a hand as she reached the top. "And the best part is this!" He jumped off the rock screaming, "Geronimo!" until he hit the water with a smack.

David looked at Sarah. "I'm a little scared to make the jump," he admitted. "You know me and heights."

"No problem," she said as she made a gesture towards the rope for the trek down. Seeing David considering it, she grabbed David's hand and jumped off the rock face.

David had no choice but to follow her lead, though he screamed like a school girl all the way down. Sarah thought she could even still hear him screaming under water. She popped up first and then came David sputtering, his eyes wide open like they were ready to pop out of his head.

"That was mean," he said to his wife, "but I am glad you did it. That was a scream."

"I know!" Sarah laughed. "Literally!"

"Oh you think so, eh?" David joked as he grabbed her around the waist and dragged her under.

By this time Zane was half way up the slope. "You guys coming again?" he called out.

"We sure are!" David shouted.

After several trips up and down the rock face, Zane said, "That's about all I can do for now."

"I'm with you," Sarah said. "My muscles are starting to complain."

"Come on," David coerced. "One more jump; you can do it."

"Okay, okay, one more jump," the others agreed.

All three got to the top, held hands, and jumped, yelling "Geronimo!" as they kicked and twisted on the way down to the water's surface. The swim back to the boat seemed longer for all three as their muscles were done from climbing.

Back on board Zane said, "Let's get changed. I've some snacks for the ride home."

When Sarah and David were dried and dressed, they made their way back to the deck. Zane already had a bag of Ruffles chips and a tube of Hillary's dip out, along with three ice cold Cokes.

"This is perfect," David beamed. "I could use some refreshment after all the exercise."

"I thought you would," Zane replied as the captain pulled up the anchor and they headed back to the town dock.

Sarah pulled out her journal as she could see Zane was in the mood for another financial talk. "If all these great investments are out there, why don't more people know about and invest in them?" she asked.

"Another great question, Sarah." Zane acknowledged as he put a large chip into his mouth and began chewing.

Sarah waited patiently.

"It's like this," he said finally when his mouth was empty. "Many people have never picked up a nonfiction book to learn something since they left high school. Many people are living day to day, week to week in survival mode, and the idea of living on less to save some money or getting a temporary second job or a raise to earn more money to save is not were they're at. It's easy to do and easy not to do. Many people don't think they have enough to invest, so they never grow it into more. Some would like to but don't qualify for the investments."

"What do you mean don't qualify?" Sarah asked.

"Each province is different so check with your professional. The last time I checked in Ontario, you need to be a sophisticated investor to qualify."

"What's a sophisticated investor?" David asked.

Zane smiled and looked up as he tried to recall the criteria. "It goes something like this. You need to qualify under one of the following provisions. The first way you could is you must invest $150,000 or more in one investment and it must not be your only investment. The second way you could is you must have a personal yearly income of $200,000 or more for the last two years. The third way is you must have a yearly family income of $300,000 or more for the last two years. Or finally, the fourth is you could have a net worth excluding your personal residence of $1,000,000 or more. This can include face value of life insurance policies. If you meet one of these criteria, you can invest in just about anything. The beauty with real estate is you just have to be 18 years or older, have some downpayment, and qualify for the mortgage."

"Those are pretty tough requirements to be a sophisticated investor," David said.

"Yes, they are. I guess the Ontario government is concerned with protecting undereducated investors from these less liquid, high return investments. Some provinces follow Ontario's lead while others have less stringent or no rules to qualify. So, if you ever relocate or have friends or relatives in other provinces, the folks that sell the different investments are well educated in what is required."

"I see," said Sarah. "Where did you find out about these great investments?"

"I learned some from reading, from my investment advisor, from seminars, and most I learned from joining a wealth building club. It is an education club that has a neat program. Club members meet once a month to discuss wealth building ideas and to encourage one another. There are also opportunities to do due diligence trips to exotic places. That's how I got my hotel and food paid for while in Belize. The company doing the investment paid for a qualified investors. All I had to do was pay for my airfare."

"It's rough for the wealthy, isn't it?" David joked.

"Yes, yes it is." Zane joked back.

"Is that all there is to it?" Sarah asked.

"No," Zane replied. "It is just the start. There is lots of learning to do. Remember I said to spend fifteen minutes a day or one hour a week learning and monitoring your wealth? As you become more educated, you'll get wiser and make better investment decisions. It's so easy and yet so difficult for most. You know, easy to do, easy not to do. I have even written a book so that I can spread the word."

"That's so cool," David marveled. "You writing a book and all."

"Yes it is," Zane beamed. "I've been collecting knowledge for the past thirty years and finally committed to putting it down. I hired a book coach to get me started, researched publishers, and started writing. Once I got started, it really flowed. It only took me a year of work on a part time basis. I got a lot done when I went on holidays because the other things that normally distracted me weren't present."

"I'm so excited to read your book!" Sarah exclaimed. "Will you autograph it for me?"

"It will be my pleasure once it is printed," Zane smiled.

Just then the captain slowed the boat as they had arrived back at the main dock. "Here we are, back safe and sound," Zane said.

Sarah and David went below to collect their things before disembarking. As they were leaving and saying their good byes, the couple thanked Zane over and over for his hospitality and the information he had imparted to them.

All Zane could say was, "It was my pleasure. It was a blessing to give." Then he paused. "Wait, hold on a second."

Zane went below and found the proof copy of his new book and autographed it: "To one of the funnest couples I know and to the best students I have ever had. May you read this book in good wealth. Your friend, Zane."

Sarah kissed Zane on the cheek and hugged him, and David also hugged him.

"Thanks again!" they called to their friend as he headed back to the boat. The couple unlocked the bike, loaded their overnight pack into the carrier, and hopped on the shiny bicycle for the trek home.

It was just getting dark when they road into the driveway of the little home in Brinston. As they got off the bike Sarah kidded with David, "I'm ahead of you! I'm ahead of you.!"

"What do you mean?" David retorted.

"I'm already a quarter of the way through the book. I read while we paddled home."

"I wondered why you were so quiet," David mused.

Sarah laughed, and they went inside. "I'm not sure yet," she said, "but I think the book is about us."

"You mean about a couple like us," David asked.

"No, I mean about us. I think we're the couple in the book," Sarah said with a tear appearing in the corner of her eye.

After dinner Sarah caught herself looking lovingly into David's eyes. She had never felt the urge so strongly before. Maybe it was her insecurity with their finances that stopped her before, or maybe now she was just ready.

David gave her a puzzled look.

She smiled and winked at him as she grabbed his hand. "Want to go make a baby?" she asked temptingly.

David's eyes lit up, not just because he was going to get lucky tonight, but because Sarah as usual was unwittingly able to clarify for him what he wanted most in life.

"I thought you'd never ask," David grinned boyishly as he picked up his bride in his strong arms and carried her upstairs.

Saturday

What a beautiful day on the boat!
Breakfast was great.

Zane's Advice:
- Work on my investment
  portfolio and learn about
  investments for at least one
  hour per week
- Register for a TFSA for
  David and myself in a financial
  company that can also hold
  RRSP funds
- Different investments are
  REIT's, MIC's, and second
  mortgages
- Buying an investment property
  every five years is a great
  investment strategy. Let's pay
  down our mortgage as fast
  as possible so we can buy
  our first investment property
- The power of leverage is
  amazing! It is possible to get
  an average of 18% in a stable
  market

- Look for a great investment
advisor and a tax adviser
- Investigate RESP for when
we have children!

MY DECISIONS AND ACTION ITEMS.

What is the next financial book I will read?

Is real estate investing an option for me?

How much equity do I have in my house?

Who is my real estate professional that I will use for investment properties?

To pay it forward, who are at least two people I will buy *The Wealth Formula* for?

PUTTING IT INTO OVER DRIVE

Several days went by, each ending with David and Sarah reading a chapter in Zane's book every night before bed. Friday came, and Sarah was feeling sick to her stomach. "I'm not feeling well David, I think I have to call in sick from work today"

"Do you need me to stay home with you?" David asked.

Sarah didn't answer his question as she darted to the bathroom. David reiterated, "So, you want me to stay at home with you?"

"No," Sarah responded, hunched over the toilet, "I'm not that sick; I'm only nauseous. I called my mom, and she asked if I possibly could be pregnant because my symptoms sound like morning sickness."

"Let's hope so," David said and leaned over to kiss Sarah on the forehead. "I have to go to work now. Call me on my work phone if you need me."

"Okay, I will," Sarah called weakly. "Have a good day at work."

After David left, Sarah couldn't help herself. She was curled up in bed trying to ignore the pains in her stomach, and the book Zane had written was calling out to her. 'David will forgive me for going ahead,' she thought to herself.

As she picked up the book she realized that they were on the last chapter. She read the title out loud, "Overdrive."

This chapter is all about others. You may have thought building wealth is all about you, and in some ways it is. As Yoda said in Star Wars, "There is no try; you only do or do not." Since you are reading this chapter, you are a doer. Remember back to the four levels that all started with an "S."

Survival is week to week.

Stability is one months expenses in an emergency fund.

Success is 3-6 months in expenses in an emergency fund and no consumer debt.

Significance is 1 year expenses in an emergency fund and 12 years of expenses invested.

Once you have hit significance, it is time to kick your giving into overdrive. With twelve years expenses invested in great investments, you might be saying, 'Why should I keep working? I can retire now and live the good life.' Don't do it! The average life expectancy after retirement is short. Keep working at what you love, work for free, volunteer, donate all your income to charity, but keep things in your life that you are passionate about.

There are some things that if you have not already completed, it's time to take care of them. The first is to prearrange your funeral. I know this sounds morbid, but it makes a very stressful time for family a little less stressful when all the decision are made. However, don't prepay for your funeral. This is a waste of money; you will have lots to pay it with when you die. It is better that you make money with your money than the funeral home make money on your money. You can pre decide things like cremation or burial, type of casket, funeral home, types of service, burial location etc. Some even pick the songs they would like sung or whether they want an open or closed casket. You maybe even want to record a short goodbye to your family and friends on audio or DVD.

Okay, I know you are thinking this is way too depressing. Let's move on to more fun topics. I taught earlier about RESP's, Registered Education Savings Plans; now may be a good time to review that section of the book. Having children is one way we can be significant. We can provide for them, help educate them emotionally, spiritually, and mentally so that they are able to continue the legacy you have begun to build. A short warning here: Do not pass on too much wealth to a child who is not ready for the responsibility. Make sure you train up your child in the way of the wealthy so he or she will not be too stingy or reckless with the gift you are leaving behind. For them, and for their children, and their children's children.

Next, estate planning is important any time in life, and yet it becomes more important as you accumulate more wealth and as you age. Death can come at any time, yet the probability increases as we age. Estate planning should eliminate any argument about what is to happen with your assets and will limit the taxes payable by the estate. This is good planning which will allow you to tell where you want your hard earned money to go to. I would do this ASAP, unless you would like the government to get a large share of your estate.

A family trust is an excellent way for you to transfer wealth out of a company to your family without it being taxed in your hands first. This should be set up early if possible in a corporation's life before there is a large value or any value in the shares. Basically, your lawyer and accountant can set this up, and your children do not need to know about it. You will need three trustees and a witness. Two of the trustees can be the spouses. Two trustees can declare a dividend on these special class of shares so that money from the corporation can go to the trust members in whatever amount you want, and it is taxable income in the hands of the receiver at the preferred dividend tax rate. This could be a great way to top off RESP money for your adult student, or for a down payment gift, or you just may way want to enjoy seeing how they react and treat this 'found' money. A great way is to test with a little before you entrust them with much.

A higher risk type of investment is flow thought shares. For high income earners who don't need any more money, this is an interesting option. You could say invest $100,000 into a mining partnership. See your EMR, Exempt Market Representative, for access to this type of investment. It is called a flow through share because the government wants exploration and recognizes that in the first year or so of exploration, it is all expenses and no income. The government allows the exploration company to pass through these expenses to the share holders, so the person investing $100,000 will receive a reduction in their taxes at their maximum rate. If that is 42%, you will receive $42,000 back in taxes. Your investment then has a book value of zero instead of $100,000 because you have written it off. There are even government incentives so you could receive back an additional 10%, or $10,000, so that you are at 52% of your investment back. The investment must remain for a minimum of 18 months, at which time you can do what you like with the shares.

It is important to know that they may be worthless if there was no minerals discovered. One way to mitigate this risk is to invest in a partnership that has multiple companies within it, so there is more chance of a mineral discovery.

Let's say for instance that after two years the shares are worth the same as you paid for them, $100,000. If you were to cash them in, you would create a tax requirement of capital gains tax on $100,000 because they have a zero book value. If you wanted to donate the money, you could get a tax break on what is left to donate, or you can donate the shares directly and you do not realize the tax gain and receive a donation credit for the current value of the assets you are donating. This, by the way, works for any stocks or shares your may own that have appreciated in value from their book value. If they have lost value from the book value, there is no gain to transfer them directly. You can sell them, book the loss, and then donate the cash if you wish. Back to my example of the $100,000 in value. You can donate the shares to charity and receive another 42% tax credit from the government. You have now received 94% back, so it has directly cost you 6% or $6,000 to donate $100,000.

This is where the fun begins. There are charities out there that are basically trust charities. They can act as a broker for a small fee if you want to donate shares to a charity that does not have the ability to receive a non cash donation. The best part is they have the ability to receive asset of funds into a fund in which they manage the money to try to grow it. You then can donate the proceeds on a yearly basis and your initial donation remains in the foundation. The money must remain in here for at least ten years before they can be dispensed fully or partially to charities. Three percent each year from the growth to a charity or charities of your choice must be distributed. This is a way to pool your charity money into a dowry fund and receive the tax savings right away but assign amounts out in the future. You may be asking 'Why?' or 'Who cares? Why not just give the money to the charity now?' This system is a perfect way to leave a legacy behind. For instance, you may want a certain amount to go to charity for as long as the money lasts. This could be forever if the asset is managed well and the amount given each year is below the growth of the asset each year. This is a great way to set up a scholarship program for certain students to receive money. You can set up the criteria used to select the student for university or trade school. It may be used to sponsor families or farming in another country. The choice is totally yours as long as it goes to a registered charity.

May God be with you as you journey through this life,

Zane.

When David got home, Sarah had tears in her eyes. "What's wrong?" he exclaimed, pulling her into a hug. "You said you would call me if you had a problem or were worse off."

"It's not that I am feeling sick," Sarah explained, "I feel fine. I read ahead of where we were in the book to the end. I'm now positive that the book was written for us."

"Of course it feels that way," David comforted her. "Zane was teaching us all the principles from his book, so it feels like it was for us."

"David, you just don't get it," she continued. "Call it a gut feeling or a God incident. The last chapter reminded us to look into RESP (Registered Education Savings Plans). The timing is perfect with us planning to have children."

"I see," said David, thinking the pregnancy hormones were already kicking in.

Sarah continued, "Not only that, our dream of setting up a scholarship at the church for youth to go to college or university is explained in the last chapter. You will need to read it yourself to see what I mean." She sat down on a chair slowly and shook her head. "I also keep getting this feeling that we won't see Zane again."

"I hope that's not true," David replied. Sorrow bit into the pit of his stomach. He sat down beside her. "I hope you're wrong," he said softly. "Then again, remember, Zane said some friendships are for a lifetime and some are for a season." He put his arms around her, and they sat there silently for what seemed like hours.

Days turned into weeks, weeks into months, and months turned into years. Although they would go out on the bicycle built for two as often as they could for at least the first couple of years, they would never run into Zane again. David and Sarah each planned trips where they had met Zane before and yet never saw sign of him. David checked regularly for Zane's book to come out on the market but never could find it. One problem was he didn't know the title as their copy didn't have one and Zane could have used a different name to publish under. To solve this, David and Sarah read every new financial book that came out on the market. Year after year they read book after book, honing their financial skills while looking for the perfect book Zane had written.

They never did find the book. Each year Sarah and David would take a vacation and rent a boat on the same weekend that they had had that wonderful experience with Zane. They would reminisce on what a great mentor Zane had become and wish they could see him again. David loved this weekend on the boat each year. He would bring their financial net worth statement, and he and Sarah would look at what they had accomplished on their bucket list and add to it as they dreamed and planned their goals for the following year.

One memorable year, Sarah said to David, "I can't believe how many things we've accomplished on our lists."

"I know," replied David. "I have about forty five things highlighted out of the now one hundred and five items. Like the owning of sixteen investment properties. In only twenty short years, we've accomplished forty five major things in our lives."

"I know," said Sarah, "I've about another twenty items highlighted that weren't on your list. Like going to Israel. That means we've been doing an average of three things a year and having a family at the same time."

"We sure have," David said as he reflected on how quiet it was without the four kids with them. "It's so nice that Mike and Ruth take the kids for this weekend every year. You know, I really appreciate all that your parents have and continue to do for us, Sarah."

"I agree," Sarah replied. "Between my parents and Zane, they have been the most influential and inspirational people in our lives."

"Amen to that," David acknowledged as he pulled the boat up to the lake house dock. They really had to concentrate to dock the thirty eight foot cruiser. It was not like driving their eighteen foot bow rider.

Once David and Sarah had secured the boat, they headed up to the lake house that Michael and David had built together on Lac St. Marie. David and Michael had purchased some investments in the development of Lac St. Marie and from the proceeds purchased a waterfront lot.

David poured Sarah and himself a tall, cold glass of iced tea, and they sat down to wait for Michael, Ruth, and their four children to arrive. They were sitting on the screened in porch watching the sun set across the lake. Sarah broke the silence. "You know something, David? I pulled out my ultimate scenario letter the other day, and I don't think our lives thus far could have gotten any closer to my ultimate scenario. It's like everything I wrote on paper has been realized in real life."

"That's so cool," David said as he rubbed her back with one arm and took another sip of his drink with the other. "We are truly blessed, and I thank God for all he has done for us."

"I sure do," said Sarah. "It's amazing to know that our work in Kenya is coming to an end. Kenya now produces so much food, they're supplying other parts of Africa with it." Her ears perked up as she heard the sound of tires on the gravel.

She bounced out of her chair because, although she loved her weekend alone with David rereading Zane's book every year, she also loved her four children dearly, missed them tremendously, and couldn't wait to give them all hugs and kisses when they arrived with Grandma and Grandpa.

<u>Saturday</u>

It's been over fifteen years since we last saw Zane. I still believe he wrote the book for David and I. I hope we will see him again, but I have a feeling we won't. I guess some friends and mentors are only for a season.

It's amazing how much my life is now almost exactly like what I wrote in my ultimate scenario letter. And so many things are highlighted on my Bucket List. Whenever we come to the lakehouse, and I sit on the porch watching the kids play in the water, I shudder to think what our lives would be like without the lessons learned from Zane and the wealth formula! I am just so grateful...

What am I grateful for?

What do I need to complete from previous chapters?

What am I grateful for?

THE BIG SURPRISE

The next week, it was all back to normal, so to speak. There was work to do, properties to manage, charities to help run, kids to watch and see off to school, sporting events, and so on. Sarah decided that for her husband's forty fifth birthday she was going to buy him something really meaningful, something on his bucket list.

Sarah started looking on EBay week after week but was starting to run out of time as David's birthday was only four weeks away. Every night Sarah would go on online looking at the new listings, and then she finally found the item she was looking for. It was a silver Maserati Spyder with red leather interior and a six speed manual transmission. The car was in fantastic shape for being around twenty five years old. She noted someone must have really cared for this car to keep it in such good condition, and the paint shone like it had just come out of the show room. "What a beauty," she mumbled to herself. It was perfect for what she wanted. Now all she had to do was win the bidding war on EBay. The auction was a no reserve auction with a five day length.

Sarah had found quite a number of excellent buys over the years as she had become very frugal with the money they made. She figured every dollar saved was one she could invest or donate. Every day Sarah watched the price of the little car climb as people put in their bids to try to make the purchase of their life on EBay.

On day three, the car was at $20,000 US dollars. The assent seemed to be slowing as some bidders dropped out. On day four, she opened her account to watch what was happening, and the little car that was soon to be an antique was at $24,500 US dollars. Sarah knew that money was not an issue as she and David had recently surpassed the $4,000,000 net worth mark just like Zane had said they would.

Day five and the Maserati was up to $40,000. The car was now worth about $45,000 according to Sarah's research, and because it was exactly what she had been wanting, she was willing to pay up to $55,000 for the little roadster. The bidding was going to end at 10:30 p.m. that night and she had still not placed a bid yet. Sarah quickly shut down the computer as she saw David's car coming up the driveway to their luxury five bedroom home in Manotick. Sarah thought back to all the dumps they had lived in that they renovated and sold one to two years later each time. It was such a blessing that they now lived in this beautiful home with a view of the Rideau River.

Sarah was startled out of her day dream as the front door swung open and David hollered, "Daddy is home!" She heard the kids' doors open as all four ran to give their father a big hug and a kiss.

David threw his arms around the two youngest and attempted to pick them all up, when he fell over and they piled on top to roughhouse him. Sarah just smiled as this had become a routine at their home, and she would patiently wait for her turn. Sometimes if she was a little too close, David would get an arm free and grab her leg to pull her into the pile. After several minutes of laughter, giggles, and screams of delight, David freed himself from the pile up and swooped Sarah into his arms. After a ten second kiss, he asked Sarah, "Did I tell you I love you today?"

"Oh, David," she replied. "You know, it has been a long day, maybe you should tell me again."

"Okay," David smiled as his tone became serious. "I love you."

"How much?" she queried innocently.

"This much!" he declared as he dropped her on the couch and spread his arms as far apart as they could go.

After dinner, they got onto the subject of David and Sarah's first home. David's slightly exaggerated stories of that old fixer upper had been told many times before, and the kids loved hearing about where the couple had been when they first started out, the old house that smelled of mice and held treasures in the loft area, the bicycle built for two, picnics by the water, and the chance meeting with Zane. All four could tell you everything about Zane, although none had ever met him. The couple had taught the kids all the wisdom Zane had imparted to them about money. Sarah also had created some very unique money systems for them so that they would hopefully not make the errors their parents had made as they became adults. Sarah knew that the largest part of creating lasting generational wealth was to pass on the wisdom that she and David had acquired over the years about money management and wealth accumulation. This was even more important than passing on the actual money.

After several stories and laughs around the table, the kids went to do their homework while David and Sarah caught up.

By ten, David was ready for bed since 5:30 comes early. He scratched his leg and yawned sleepily, asking Sarah to come to bed. Sarah replied, "I'll be up soon. You go on without me." She knew that if she stayed back, David would be asleep minutes after hitting the pillow.

Sarah quietly turned on the computer and opened her EBay account. She selected 'My EBay' and up came the Maserati. The little car was now at $41,000 Sarah noticed, as the time on the auction counted down. At five minutes, $41,200. At three minutes, $41,500. One minute, $42,000. Thirty seconds, $42,400. Sarah typed in her bid of $55,000 and with seven seconds left hit the 'Send' button. She knew she may pay up to $55,000 for the car and yet no one would have time to type in a bid to out bid her. Only pre-programmed maximum bids would have a chance.

Sarah giggled with delight as the computer screen displayed: "Congratulations You Just Won." She looked at the number and was pleased; she had won the auction bid at $43,100. Sarah knew she would still have shipping duty and taxes to pay to get the little car into Canada. She paid the deposit required and decided she would arrange for shipping and payments the following day. She quietly slipped into bed beside her snoring husband and lay awake thinking about how excited David would be on his birthday.

The next morning Sarah went about her usual schedule and then around 10:00am called the shipping broker to make arrangements for delivery of the car on David's birthday. She then headed off to the money exchange to verify the exchange rate. She and David had bought other used cars in the USA before and she was familiar with the process of getting a car into Canada. Last time they bought a car and went to the exchange for the money they saved over $500 over using the bank. She realized that fortunately David's birthday was going to be on a Saturday this year, so all the kids could be home to join the excitement.

The days seemed to slow down to a halt as she waited for David's big birthday surprise. Email after email came to her on the status of the car. First it was payment received, then paperwork shipped to the border, then the car shipped to the border. A few days before David's birthday, the dealership in Montreal called to say they had received the car and would start the process to modify the car to meet Canadian standards. They said it would be shipped out on Saturday for a Saturday delivery. The email reminded Sarah that there was an extra hundred dollar charge to deliver the car on the weekend and that they had put the giant red bow on the car as she had requested. Sarah smiled as her plan was coming together perfectly.

Early Saturday morning while David was sleeping in, Sarah got up with the kids and made breakfast early. They were all going to pretend that they didn't remember it was David's birthday. They all knew the party would begin when the present arrived. She put her finger to her lips as she heard David's footsteps coming down the stairs. The others laughed.

David walked into the kitchen with a large smile on his face. "Good morning!" he chirped as he kissed the kids and then lingered to kiss Sarah.

Several of the younger ones began making gagging sounds and told their parents to get a room. They always put up a fuss and yet they loved how their parents loved each other and that they openly showed their affection for each other, even after many years of marriage.

As David sat down at the table for what he assumed would be a family meal, Sarah broke his thoughts, "The kids and I have some errands to run. The boys need something in town and Jane needs something at a friend's house. We'll be back around noon. We've already eaten, so you just need to get your own breakfast. Don't worry about lunch, we'll bring back groceries." Sarah motioned for the teens to get up and she gave David a kiss on the forehead. "Oh, I almost forgot," she said as she pulled a piece of paper out of her tight jeans.

David grinned as he admired how great she looked after four children and all these years. The grin quickly faded as she handed him a Honey-Do list. With a lot of things on it.

Sarah smiled, "I think you can get most of it done before we get back." Before he could protest, she and the kids scurried out the door and piled into the extended Escalade.

David watched as his family pulled out of the driveway. The smile disappeared off of his face as he remembered the long list and the fact that no one had given much thought about him. As the day went on and he checked one item after another off the list, he got more and more frustrated. How could they forget his birthday and then leave him with such a long, boring laundry list of things to do?

Meanwhile, Sarah and the kids were bursting. They drove into the city to buy a birthday cake, a case of Coke, chicken and wedges from the grocery store, and a giant birthday card. Ruth and Michael met up with Sarah and the kids around 11:30 a.m.; she had already filled them in on the big surprise.

Sarah and the kids arrived just before noon, smiling and laughing jovially. She pulled David aside to cheerfully see the things he had done while the kids unloaded the car and hid the cake and card. Ruth and Mike were parked a block away, waiting patiently for the car to arrive. Shortly after noon, the car transport truck parked in front of the home with Sarah's parents right behind it. The truck driver hit the air horn a few times.

David grumpily put down a wrench and pulled his head out of the bathtub he was changing the faucet in for Sarah. "I wonder what that's all about on a Saturday?" he grumbled.

Sarah hid her smirk by turning her back. She was doing everything she could to suppress a giggle. Normally, she would have felt sorry for him being so unhappy, but today she found his grumbling hilarious. "Are the neighbours moving today? Maybe you should go and check it out."

David reluctantly went outside to find an enclosed car transport truck and Ruth and Michael parked in his driveway. The driver asked his name and verified the address. "Just sign here," he said, "and I'll off load 'er." He moved to put the paperwork back into the cab.

"Off load what?" David asked, scratching his head.

The driver turned around slowly and looked at him in surprise. "Just the nicest car I've ever moved," he murmured sassily.

"What?" David was dumbfounded. "Happy Birthday!" Sarah cried out, and then everyone else shouted, "Happy Birthday!"

David was overwhelmed with emotion. He had just minutes ago been frustrated and angry that everyone had forgotten, and now he was blown away with excitement. The driver backed the car down the ramp, and David gasped as he caught a glimpse of the sports car. He turned to Sarah with wide eyes. "Is this really for me?"

Sarah just smiled and nodded her head. David ran over and spun her so many times that they almost fell onto the driveway in a dizzy pile.

What seemed like hours but was only minutes went by, and the little roadster was on the road and ready for inspection. David walked around the car and stared at it through blurry eyes. It was perfect. The driver handed the keys to David. He jumped into the driver's seat to look the car over from the inside. David thought he could still smell the leather seats. "How did you find one exactly like Zane's car?" he asked.

Sarah just smiled. Her surprise had worked.

The driver came over to Sarah and said, "I need your signature on this document."

Sarah signed and thought nothing more of it. Then, David and Sarah heard a car exhaust that they hadn't heard in a very long time. They jerked their heads up, stunned.

The driver backed off the truck a 68 Firebird 400. It was a black beauty. As he parked the car and handed Sarah the keys, he nonchalantly said, "There you are, ma'am."

Sarah gaped in shock. "There must be some sort of mistake. I only bought one car."

"No, there's no mistake," replied the driver. "Here is the bill of lading and a letter that came with the car, addressed to a Sarah and David.

Sarah stared at the manilla envelope and tore it open with shaking hands.

'Hello to my treasured friends,

I hope you are well.

It was with mixed feelings that I put my Maserati up for sale, and imagine my joy when I saw the name of the successful bidder. It is so perfect that you two would buy my treasured little car.

I know it is best, and yet I miss that I have not connected with you for a long time. I knew you had learned all that I was able to give you, and it was time for me to continue working with others ready to start similar journeys.

After I learned that it was you who bought my car, I remembered how delighted you were to drive in my Firebird that beautiful day we picnicked by the Rideau River, and I thought who else would I rather have own my 68 Firebird than you two. Watching you both grow on your financial journey was such an encouragement to me.

So this is my personal gift to you. Please enjoy it as much as I have. And now I would like to request that you return the favour by writing a book about your journey, incorporating the teaching in the manuscript that I gave you as I never did publish the book.

I've reached the end of my teaching days in Canada and the USA. The world at large was not ready for my message when I first wrote it, and now consumer debt has increased significantly. A super low interest rate should reduce indebtedness, and yet it is just fueling consumerism. People are using their homes as ATM machines and are pulling money out every five years to pay down debt. This is no way to build generational wealth.

I am moving to Africa to continue work with YouFeedThem and to start another organization. Kenya is learning to build wealth, and surrounding countries are open to moving forward as well.

Please write the story. The time is right and the need is great!

May God bless you and keep you,

Your friend Zane

Tears streamed down Sarah and David's faces as Sarah folded up the letter.

100 THINGS TO DO

1. _______________________________
2. _______________________________
3. _______________________________
4. _______________________________
5. _______________________________
6. _______________________________
7. _______________________________
8. _______________________________
9. _______________________________
10. _______________________________
11. _______________________________
12. _______________________________
13. _______________________________
14. _______________________________
15. _______________________________
16. _______________________________
17. _______________________________
18. _______________________________
19. _______________________________
20. _______________________________
21. _______________________________

22. ____

23. ____

24. ____

25. ____

26. ____

27. ____

28. ____

29. ____

30. ____

31. ____

32. ____

33. ____

34. ____

35. ____

36. ____

37. ____

38. ____

39. ____

40. ____

41. ____

42. ____

43. ____

44. ____

45. ____

46. ____

47. ____

48. ____

49. ____

50. ____

51. ____

52. ____

53. ____

54. ____

55. ____

56. ____

57. ____

58. ____

59. ____

60. ____

61. ____

62. ____

63. ____

64. ____

65. ____

66. ____

67. ____

68. ____

69. ____

70. ____

71. ____

72. ____

73. ____

74. ____

75. ____

76. ____

77. ____

78. ____

79. ____

80. ____

81. ____

82. ____

83. ____

84. ____

85. ____

86. ____

87. ____

88. ____

89. ____

90. ____

91. ____

92. ____

93. ____

94. ____

95. ____

96. ____

97. ____

98. ____

99. ____

100. ____